Praise for Shadowing St. Francis

"In Shadowing St. Francis, Jonathan Bentley invites readers on a pilgrimage of faith that is at once personal, philosophical, and profoundly hopeful. His narrative embodies the open-and-relational vision of a God who persuades through love rather than control, and his storytelling gives theology a human face. A beautiful contribution to the growing conversation about emergent faith in our time."

Thomas Jay Oord, author of *God Can't: How to Believe in God and Love after Tragedy, Abuse, and Other Evils*

"Jonathan Bentley's pilgrimage journey is an invitation to those of us navigating the uncertain terrain between deconstruction and reconstruction. With honesty and grace, he shows us that the erosion of certainty isn't a loss of faith but an opening toward something more spacious and true. This is a book for question-askers and those who suspect that the gospel might be wider and wilder than we've been told. Shadowing St. Francis reminds us that faith isn't about having all the answers—it's about learning to walk with deeper questions."

Keri Ladouceur, Executive Director & Co-Founder - Post Evangelical Collective

"This book is what happens when theology steps out of abstraction and onto the road. Jonathan shows how faith can move beyond rivalry, beyond the mimetic pull toward power or certainty, into something freer—a consent to love, to mystery, to one another. It's thoughtful, disarming, and exactly the kind of story the church needs right now."

Jonathan Foster, author of *indigo: the color of grief*

"Here is an engaging story that reminds us you cannot think your way to God. In this pilgrimage across Italy ideas are not argued but lived; textured with doubt, humor, longing, and faith. A courageous and spacious account of reconstruction. Jonathan's writing invites us to think with our hearts as much as our minds, to remember that the gospel was never a theory but a life shared."

Samantha Beach Kiley, co-author of *Next Sunday: An Honest Dialogue About the Future of the Church*

SHADOWING ST. FRANCIS

A Pilgrimage *of* Sacred Emergence *in the* Age of AI

JONATHAN BENTLEY

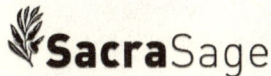

Hardcover: 978-1-968136-38-3
Paperback: 978-1-968136-37-6
Ebook: 978-1-968136-35-2

Printed in the United States of America

Library of Congress Cataloguing-in-Publication Data
Shadowing St. Francis: A Pilgrimage of Sacred Emergence in the Age of AI /
Jonathan Bentley

For Judy,

my wife of over 40 years,
who watched me venture into the wilderness
and never doubted I'd return.

Table of Contents

Author's Note

This book is based on a pilgrimage along the Way of Saint Francis that I took with three friends in the spring of 2023. The journey itself—the miles walked and the spiritual discoveries—was true to the struggles I was having at the time.

For narrative clarity, conversations have been compressed, reorganized, or expanded. The theological and philosophical exchanges reflect real discussions that occurred before, during, and after the pilgrimage, but many are placed at specific points in the story to shape a coherent arc.

The friends who accompanied me are real people, and I have sought to stay faithful to their personalities while expanding dialogue to bring the book's central questions into sharper focus. Franco, the wiry Italian porter who transported our luggage between overnight stays, is also real—true to his physical description and character—though I have placed in his mouth a range of wisdom and spiritual insight I've been blessed to receive from a handful of counselors over my deconstruction journey.

One exception to this approach: Jules, the astrophysicist I meet on the plane to Paris, and David, the investment banker I meet on the train to Florence, are composite characters. They are not portraits of any single person, living or dead. I created them to wrestle with ideas that were reshaping my faith: Jules helped me imagine the universe as still unfolding rather than already finished, and David forced me to confront the contradiction of claiming God is all-powerful and all-loving in a world filled with so much random suffering and senseless tragedy.

All of the major events actually happened—from collapsing on that first brutal climb to hearing the choral chanting of monks filter down from the cathedral above into the grotto where Francis's tomb rests, from standing in St. Peter's Square as Pope Francis delivered the Angelus prayer to staring up, breathless, at the Sistine Chapel ceiling. In my absence, my wife had her own adventure finding a trapper to dispatch the family of progressive beavers deconstructing the hedge that marks the boundary of our property. The story sounds like it's made up for comic relief, but it was not. The anchor event around which we scheduled our journey—the Springsteen concert—took place on May 21, 2023, when seventy thousand people gathered on that massive ancient Roman chariot track, the Circus Maximus.

I wrote every word in this book. But I didn't write it alone.

ChatGPT was released just months prior to our pilgrimage in the spring of 2023. Its arrival shaped not only how I would later write this book but the journey itself. That's why I chose to include a handful of reconstructed chat sessions in the narrative—to make visible how AI became part of my theological wrestling, not just an abstract concept but a real interlocutor helping me think through questions I couldn't answer alone.

Throughout the writing process, I used AI as a research assistant and thought partner. When I needed to verify a historical detail, explore theological concepts, or understand technical frameworks, AI helped me research in minutes what once took days. When struggling to articulate a complex idea, I generated multiple variations, each attempt teaching me what I was trying to say.

My father and grandfather were both builders, so it was natural for me to think of this new technology as something like what power tools did for carpenters. The tools accelerate the work—what once took days now takes hours. But the carpenter still chooses every cut, every join, every finish. The craftsmanship remains entirely human; the tools simply remove friction from the process.

I wrestle with the ethical implications. These AI systems were trained, in part, on text created by authors who never consented to their work becoming training data. I support efforts to create fairer compensation models and believe regulation is both necessary and coming. In the meantime, I use these tools as I once used libraries—to research, explore possibilities, and pressure-test my ideas. Everything in the final text is my expression, my voice, my creative choices.

AI, like the friends who walked beside me, simply helped me find my way.

Prologue: Winter

It was a brittle, gusty January morning in the low forties. I sat on the back porch of our North Carolina home, staring across the creek at the bare hillside beyond. The trees were skeletal, their limbs twitching in the wind like arthritic fingers grasping at nothing. In a few months, they would bloom again with new life. But today, they looked like what they were—stripped bare by winter, vulnerable, uncertain whether the roots still held.

Looking at those naked hardwoods, I found myself thinking not only about the state of my own soul, but also about the institution I had served for over fifty years. The Church—capital C, the whole wounded, magnificent, terrible enterprise—stood just as bare before me now, its pretenses blown away by scandal after scandal, its branches brittle with legalism, its canopy no longer offering the shelter it once promised. What remained when you stripped away the prosperity gospel, the culture wars, the quest for political power? Were there roots worth saving, or had the whole thing rotted from within?

But there was something else in that winter view. I knew those branches looked dead, but I also knew they weren't—they were concealing life that was waiting to emerge.

That morning, a new and troubling question weighed on me. Six months earlier, we had welcomed our fifth grandchild into the world—Paul, the first boy after four radiant girls. Just yesterday, after our Sunday family lunch, I watched Paul's sister and cousins play together with that unrestrained enthusiasm that makes everything loud and joyful, even the tantrums. As I watched each girl practicing future parenting skills on the boy, an unexpected ache surfaced—not physical, but heart pain that caught me off guard.

It struck me suddenly: if any of them were old enough to ask me—as I hoped they would someday—"Should I be a Christian?" I wouldn't know how to answer. I had once been part of a movement that tried to reform the Church from within—the Jesus Movement of the '70s, when we thought we could change everything with bare feet, long hair, and electric guitars. We believed we were dragging Christianity into relevance, making it authentic again. But now I could see how that movement had been co-opted, how we'd ended up building the very machine that was now weaponizing scripture against the vulnerable.

The question wasn't whether the Church needed fixing—it was whether fixing was even the right metaphor. I felt as though the issues weren't about better doctrines or better behavior. It was something more fundamental. What if the problems were with the theological operating system itself—assumptions about the nature of revelation, the role of science, how we thought about reality and God's relationship to it?

A question I once could have met with certainty and conviction would now spill out muddled and conflicted. Not "Do I believe?" but "Do I want them to become part of this?"

Incidentally, I'd started playing around with ChatGPT, which had been recently released. With 20 or so years of working with decision trees and algorithms, as soon as I used it the first time I knew there was something remarkably different about this thing people were calling generative AI. It became remarkably useful in helping me figure things out, but there was something else about it I couldn't yet quite articulate. Something about how it reframed my questions rather than just answering them reminded me that maybe I'd been asking the wrong questions all along. When I'd asked it about biblical interpretation, it hadn't given me a definitive answer but had instead shown me how different traditions approached the same text.

A sudden gust came through the trees, whistling as it moved among the limbs. It wasn't playful—it was sharp, almost shrill, the kind of whistle meant to rouse you from sleep. In Scripture, the word for wind—pneuma—also means spirit and breath. The Breath of God. Was this wind calling me toward something? Or was it just wind, and was I just an old man projecting meaning onto meteorology?

I felt these overwrought questions were stirred by a call I had received the day before from Gunter, an old German friend. Literally old—we were both soon to turn seventy. We hadn't spoken in nearly a year, and he was calling to invite me to join him and two of his alpine hiking friends on a spiritual pilgrimage through Italy: The Way of Saint Francis. One hundred twenty miles of walking, from Florence to Rome, tracing the ancient roads and trails of the famous barefoot friar.

Although the idea of going to Italy for three weeks might have been attraction enough, what really drew me was thinking about how Francis had reformed the broken, heavy-handed Catholicism of his day.

It seemed as though he had discovered a different kind of reform—one that worked from the bottom up, through vulnerability rather than authority. I wondered if it held any relevance to addressing those same issues in our time.

Act I: The Foundation Cracks

"We destroy arguments and every lofty opinion raised against the knowledge of God, and take every thought captive to obey Christ."

—2 Corinthians 10:5

"The dismantling seasons of our lives are not to be feared, but embraced as the place where God's newness can emerge."

—Walter Brueggemann, *Sabbath as Resistance* (2014)

The Invitation

Judy, my patient wife of over forty-five years, joined me on the porch. She knew something was off before I said a word.

"What's on your mind?" she asked, settling into her chair.

"Sitting out here usually settles you down," she noted, "but you look troubled."

"Have you ever noticed how lifeless this view up the mountain becomes this time of year?" I said it with a tone that suggested that it disappointed me.

"It's a hill, not a mountain," she observed with familiar carefulness.

"In Florida, it would be called a mountain," I said, recalling the flat terrain of our lifelong home before retiring and moving halfway north.

"We are near the mountains, but they're half a day's drive west. Don't disrespect the real mountains by elevating this little hill beyond its station." She offered this correction with a grin. "I just want to make sure you're keeping perspective."

"Actually, what I'm thinking about is the wind," I said, my voice trailing off. "I can't tell if it's crying or calling."

"What I hear sounds like the soundtrack to a graveyard scene," she said, half-grinning. "More harsh than musical."

After a moment, I leaned forward in my chair. "Do you really understand just how broken the Church is?"

"Well, that certainly sounds more harsh than musical," she quipped.

"No, really, I'm serious," I said. "It's as dead as this view up the hillside. The Church—everything I was raised to believe was solid, trustworthy, worth passing on to the next generation. When I look at it now, I see the same thing—bare branches, dead wood, wondering what's worth saving."

My voice gained intensity. "The trends are undeniable, Judy. Church attendance in free fall, entire denominations splitting over basic moral questions, millennials and Gen Z walking away in unprecedented numbers. We're not talking about normal institutional decline—this is a fundamental crisis of credibility that's been building for decades."

She gave me a measured look. "You're sounding as apocalyptic as those preachers we both can't stand listening to."

"But this is different," I insisted, leaning forward. "This is genuinely important. The stakes couldn't be higher—"

"That's your ego talking," she interrupted gently but firmly.

The words hit like cold water. I opened my mouth to defend myself, then closed it, feeling that familiar tightness in my chest—the reflex to defend my position. Once I became defensive both the kindness of my tone and the quality of my logic deteriorated. It's when my gift for being dismissive shows most clearly.

I swallowed my pride and nodded. "You're right. I was getting defensive about my interpretation instead of just listening."

She gave me that familiar look that meant she was about to say something important. "Are you in some kind of hole? How deep are you—do I need to help pull you out?"

"More like standing at the edge of a cliff, wondering whether to jump or step back." I paused. "Gunter called yesterday."

I told her about the pilgrimage invitation. The distance. The timeline. The terrain. And my growing sense that I needed to do something radical to break free from the theological paralysis that had settled over me like winter fog.

She didn't hesitate. "Wow. That sounds incredible. You said it's over a hundred miles? Over how many days?"

"More than ten, I think. But it's not until next year."

After thinking for a moment, she said, "Then you've got time to train." Looking into the distance, she added slowly, "This could be a good chance for you to get some closure on this crisis you've been wrestling with."

"It's not just about my faith anymore," I said. "It's about whether there's anything left of the Church worth recommending to our grandchildren. Whether the whole enterprise is too corrupted to salvage, or whether Francis found something that transcends institutional failure."

"Well, right now you're stuck," she said with characteristic directness. "You can't move forward, and you can't go back. Maybe walking those ancient paths will help you find a third option."

She caught my eye. "This timidity in you is unusual. You'd usually be the one selling me on how great the idea is."

I nodded, feeling the weight of her observation. "Something about aging and shrinking boundaries. And honestly, something about not trusting my own judgment anymore. When your whole worldview gets deconstructed, you start second-guessing everything."

She looked at the bare trees swaying in the wind. "You're sixty-eight, but you sound twenty years older. You need to lean into this."

"It will mean months of training," I said quietly. "But maybe that will be good for me. The physical challenge isn't quite as intimidating as the prospect of trying to figure out whether there's anything left of Christianity worth salvaging."

"Can you think of a better place than the mountains of Italy to figure that out?" she asked. "Following in the footsteps of someone who faced the same question eight centuries ago?"

Her words settled into the space between us as another gust moved through the trees. The whistling sound came again—still shrill, still urgent, but somehow more like an invitation now.

"Francis stripped himself naked in front of the bishop and the whole town," I said, almost to myself. "Gave back everything—his clothes, his inheritance, his family name. Started over with nothing but his trust in God."

"And you're wondering if you need to do something equally radical?"

"Maybe not naked in the town square," I said with a weak smile. "But something. Some way of breaking free from this spiritual paralysis that doesn't require abandoning faith altogether."

"Then call Gunter back," she said simply. "Tell him yes. But keep space for mystery on this journey. For the possibility that you might discover something you're not expecting."

That evening, I reached out to Gunter and gave him a tentative yes—pending a month of training to see if I could get my daily walking mileage up before committing to plane tickets and dates.

As I hung up the phone, I found myself wondering if this was how pilgrimage always begins—not with mystical visions or dramatic calls, but with a simple recognition that staying where you are is no longer bearable. That sometimes you have to walk away from everything familiar to discover what's worth keeping.

The trees were still bare across the creek, still swaying in the January wind. But for the first time in months, they looked less like symbols of death and more like promises of resurrection—stripped down to their essence, waiting for the right season to bloom again.

The wind picked up once more, whistling through the branches with what sounded almost like approval.

I listened to it for a moment, and a phrase came to mind, it could be a song lyric: *In the wind a song I hear.* Seven syllables. I tried humming it, playing with different note combinations—maybe the first few notes the same, then rising with the wind at the end.

Songwriters are often asked which comes first, the music or the words. I remembered that my process always started with the language, but the music always arrived with the words, the two braided together.

I have not written a song in years. Maybe this is the start of a new one. Maybe this journey would help me hear the music again.

Chasing the Goose

The first sign I wasn't in evangelical Kansas anymore was the program directory: over 300 "experiences" led by "co-creators," as if even the vocabulary had been liberated from traditional church-speak. Before my scheduled session I decided to walk the perimeter of the grounds to see what was happening in the various tents. It was only 8:30 a.m., but the August heat already pressed down, and without the sweatband in my ball cap I'd have been mopping my brow even at this early hour.

"The Wild Goose Festival has been bringing together thousands of progressive Christians each summer for nearly 15 years, creating a four-day space where spirituality meets social justice, music, and art." Joy Wallace, one of the festival's founders, de- scribes it as "either your first step in or your last step out of Christianity." She is married to veteran activist and author Jim Wallis, who has been writing about serious social engagement for most of my life. Joy explained that their goal was to create something like a mash-up of England's famous Greenbelt Festival—where she was from—and Burning Man out west. I didn't see any enormous wooden "Man" ready to be set on fire, but otherwise they seemed to have nailed it.

I looked around at all these people—wounded, questioning, searching. I wasn't alone in hearing this song. Something was emerging here, something bigger than any of us individually. I continued walking around the perimeter, pulled out my phone to look at the digital schedule, and was immediately reminded of the intimidating number of options. I looked around at all these people—wounded, questioning, searching. I wasn't alone in hearing this song. Something was emerging here, something bigger than any of us individually.

As I walked through the maze of tents, I found myself humming that melody I had settled on for the new song I began working on at home a few months earlier. Another lyric came to mind. Good next line: If you can hear it, I think it's near.

The sheer variety of options made choosing difficult—from mainstage keynotes to intimate conversations in the "Convo Tents"where tables of eight tackled everything from mysticism to social justice. My first choice was a session titled When Faith Becomes Fascism: The Dangerous Marriage of Christianity and Nationalism. As I took my seat I noted the fun, engaged vibe. that said, I missed the comfort of an air-conditioned sanctuary— the proper setting, in my old evangelical imagination, for a Christian conference.

I had read that several speakers here were branded heretics by my former gatekeepers. Maybe heretics couldn't afford air-conditioned sanctuaries.

From the handful of conversations I'd had so far, most people seemed suspended somewhere between first step and last— much like me. I'd discovered the festival while searching for events featuring Brian McLaren, the former evangelical pastor and author whose books, over the past decade, had helped me imagine a more progressive faith that takes social justice seriously and is comfortable questioning the old certainties about scripture and doctrine.

Now retired, with time finally in my own hands, I wanted to hear him in person. He was leading a writers' workshop here, and I hoped it might spark the creative impulse that first stirred in me as an English major fifty years ago but had remained locked away ever since.

This festival wasn't just a detour; it felt like preparation. In the six months since Gunter's call I had been training for the Franciscan pilgrimage to Italy—walking five to seven miles a day, losing ten pounds, and immersing myself in medieval and Reformation church history through countless audiobooks and podcasts. I had only just begun reading about Francis, yet I already sensed in him a fellow knight-troubadour willing to confront the establishment with courage and creativity—a spirit I could feel bubbling up all around me at Wild Goose.

The more I learned about Francis's approach, the more I saw parallels to what progressive Christianity was trying to accomplish. Like Francis, we were trying to fix a broken Church, but we had tools he never had access to—modern scholarship, historical perspective, broader communication networks. The stakes were much higher too, considering the millions that had walked away from the Church throughout the West in just the previous decade.

As I walked through the warren of tents and pavilions, I was struck by how different this felt from the polished evangelical events I'd known. No projected slides or celebrity pastors on well-lit stages. Instead, poets and activists gripped sheets of paper and tapped foam-ball microphones, dealing with feedback and the predictable "Can you hear me?"

The demographic was unmistakable—more than half the crowd appeared to be my age or older, their vintage tie-dye and peasant dresses marking this as a reunion of sorts. Looking at these graying former radicals, I recognized my own generation—people who had once believed we could change the world through a rebellion of spirit.

As I moved between sessions, I caught fragments of conversation that crystallized why I'd come: "... spent thirty years in therapy undoing what Sunday school taught me about shame ..." "... my kids won't even discuss religion anymore because of what they saw growing up ..." "... if one more person tells me God needed blood to forgive sin, I might actually scream ..."

These weren't abstract theological debates. These were survivors comparing wounds.

Over the course of the day there would be other mind-bending sessions: The Prosperity Gospel's War on the Poor and Weaponized Purity: How Sexual Shame Destroys Souls. The programming would have given my former church council collective apoplexy. I was oddly drawn to all of it, despite my old heresy alarm bells ringing faintly in the background.

I was in a session called The Sins of Our Evangelical Fathers—a passionate teacher systematically dismantling the theological foundations I'd grown up with. As I sat cross-legged on a blanket listening to her, I felt a welling up of righteous indignation.

"Apocalyptic theology that abandons environmental responsibility," she declared, her voice cutting through the humid air with increasing intensity. "Depravity doctrine that psychologically devastates children." Each critique landed like a perfectly aimed arrow, and I found myself nodding with increasing fervor.

When it came time for questions, a gentleman one row up and just an arm's length away raised his hand. "Dr. Patterson, I appreciate what you're saying about how all this end-times talk causes people to give up on our role here. But do I hear you saying that the hope of Jesus returning at any time to fix this shit-hole of a world around us—sorry for my language—is fundamentally wrong? You get my question, right?"

The speaker's demeanor shifted noticeably. Her face hardened, and when she responded, her voice carried an edge that hadn't been there before. "Look, we can't let nostalgic attachment to comforting fantasies prevent us from acknowledging the massive psychological and environmental damage these doctrines have caused. The research is clear on this."

The questioner tried to follow up. "But I'm asking about hope itself—"

She cut him off. "Sir, how much damage do you think is done when people are following a false hope?"

The man persisted with exasperation. "You're calling the hope of the Second Coming of Christ a false hope?"

"That's not what I'm saying," she replied, a little testy.

"It sounds to me like that's exactly what you're saying."

I watched this breakdown of such a familiar argument—one I had engaged in myself many times—and found it deeply dispiriting. I knew this argument turned on how you defined the Second Coming of Christ, but they had clearly gotten past such reasonable stages and were now both just angry. It reminded me just how much ego can distort even our most sincere attempts at truth-telling.

This was exactly what Francis had been doing eight centuries ago—calling out religious hypocrisy, challenging institutional corruption. The difference was the amplification of our cultural moment. Francis's radical witness, powerful as it was, remained largely confined to medieval Italy. We were operating in an inter-connected world where theological insights could go viral across continents, reaching millions rather than hundreds. This could very well be the kind of expanded context Jesus had envisioned when he told his disciples they would do "greater things."

This was what my Jesus People days in the 1970's seemed to lack—the intellectual firepower to challenge our own assumptions. We had regarded Hal Lindsey's The Late Great Planet Earth as serious scholarship. We didn't have authors like Brian McLaren or Rob Bell giving us bigger questions and permission to doubt in a clear and accessible way.

Later that day, I found myself in conversation with a crisis abuse counselor whose sharp eyes commanded immediate atten-tion. When I asked what had brought her to Wild Goose, her response was a quiet but intense reflection on helping people escape the psychological grip of fundamentalist theology.

"The damage goes so much deeper than most people real-ize," she said, her voice carrying the weight of countless stories. "It's not just wrong theology—it's trauma that gets passed down through generations. People spend decades trying to feel worthy of love they were taught they didn't deserve."

Her words connected directly to my Francis research. He had seen how the Church's obsession with human sinfulness destroyed people's capacity for joy and spiritual freedom. We were fighting the same battle, just with more sophisticated tools.

That evening, around a campfire with fellow pilgrims sharing exodus stories from fundamentalism, someone asked what had brought me to Wild Goose. I explained my recent freedom after selling my company, my pilgrimage preparations, my quest to figure out what remained of my Christianity. I mentioned my upcoming pilgrimage to Italy, walking from Florence to Rome, to try to figure that out.

Someone asked about my hopes for the journey, and I hadn't fully worked that out but I knew it had to do with what Francis had discovered about fixing a broken Church.

After a thoughtful silence, a woman across the fire said quietly, "Such a pilgrimage sounds wonderful, and I bet you'll learn a lot." But then almost wistfully, she added, "Our Western privilege gives us so many options that most of us just do not have."

There was something in the firelight playing across her weathered face that made me pause. I felt a little stung by the observation, but I also appreciated what it revealed about her heart for those without such options.

The silence stretched uncomfortably. Around the fire, I could see others nodding slightly—teachers, social workers, people whose freedom to attend spiritual festivals or embark on expensive pilgrimages was limited by circumstances I'd never faced. The distance between my advantages and their constraints suddenly felt vast.

I found myself stumbling over a response, something about privilege carrying obligation, but even as I said it, I knew it sounded hollow. Worse, I could feel myself getting defensive, wanting to justify my choices rather than simply acknowledge her point. That familiar tightness crept into my chest—the same reflex I'd noticed with Judy, the need to be right, to defend my position rather than just listen.

The moment passed, but it left me unsettled in a way I couldn't quite shake.

As the evening wore on and conversations swirled between confession and crusade, I found myself wondering what exactly I was witnessing. Was this gathering a kind of field hospital for those wounded by religion—souls seeking bandages and safe company—or was it a frontier outpost for those already healing, intent on building something new? Maybe it was both: the triage tent and the planning room side by side, faith deconstructing and reconstructing in the same breath. Either way, I sensed I was standing at the hinge between what had been and what might yet emerge.

We spoke of prophetic resistance, theological revolution, taking the fight directly to institutions that had wounded us. Someone passed around a petition demanding reparations from the Southern Baptist Convention. Another discussed organizing boycotts of Christian publishers who refused to platform progressive voices.

As the conversation intensified, I found myself thinking about Francis's strategic use of holy foolishness. He had understood that sometimes you have to become a "jester for God" to expose the pretensions of power.

One of the others around the fire, a man who appeared to be in his fifties, looked thoughtful but troubled as the conversation continued. "Jonathan, I appreciate your enthusiasm about finding people who ask the same questions, but I keep wondering—if we reject traditional frameworks for determining truth, how do progressive communities actually resolve disagreements? In my engineering work, when everyone defines 'quality' differently, projects collapse. What prevents this theological freedom from becoming chaos?"

Good point. In my excitement about finding people who shared my questions, I hadn't considered what happened when those questions led to different answers. The campfire fell quiet for a moment, the weight of his systematic mind pressing against my newfound enthusiasm.

Before I could respond, a younger woman to my right spoke up. I had met her earlier but had forgotten her name—I did remember she was a seminary graduate and a former pastor. "I'm not sure this addresses doctrine exactly, but someone said something to me this weekend that's been rattling around in my head. You know First Corinthians 13? The love chapter? Most people focus on the definition of love—patient, kind, all that. But what stuck with me was what Paul says remains after everything else fades. After prophecies and knowledge pass away, he says three things are left: faith, hope, and love. Not creeds. Not correct beliefs. Just . . . those three relational things."

I wasn't entirely sure of her premise, but focusing on what remains rather than what we're supposed to believe—that did reframe the passage in a way I'd never considered. The man across the fire seemed to be turning it over in his mind too, not entirely satisfied but intrigued. Something about her response had shifted the conversation—it wasn't chaos versus control, but a different kind of center altogether.

By the time I collapsed into my tent after midnight, I was drawn to the possibility of righteous warfare conducted with superior weapons. It seemed to me that the progressives had the scholarship, moral clarity, the theological high ground. Unlike my former evangelical tribe, trapped in intellectual cul-de-sacs and moral contradictions, they possessed what felt like unassailable truth.

But there was something about the man's question that nagged at me. Was there something about the very act of defending truth that inevitably corrupted it? Was the problem deeper than just having the wrong beliefs?

I drove home from the festival with a new motivation to engage, with half a dozen new books under my arm. Here, finally, were fellow rebels ready to take on the evangelical machine that seemed to have weaponized scripture. This left me wondering whether my Italian pilgrimage was less a personal spiritual quest and more like boot camp for joining that battle.

The morning after I returned, I found my thinking chair on the back porch and began the kind of slow, deliberative rocking that helped me focus. Joining me, her coffee mug in hand, Judy asked. "So how was it? You didn't share much when you got back yesterday evening."

"It's difficult to put into words," I said with a sense of hope I hadn't had in a long time. "I finally found my tribe, Judy. People asking the same questions, fighting the same battles. People who helped me understand that it's not just about personal faith—institutions and systems matter too. I always thought if individuals just got right with God, everything else would follow. But I'm learning that broken structures create broken faith, and you can't fix one without addressing the other."

She settled into her chair, and I could see her measuring her words carefully.

"You sound like you're preparing for war." That sounded harsh but I understood why she said it.

"Not war, but maybe conflict," I said. "Francis didn't politely ask the medieval Church to reform itself. Sometimes revolution requires dramatic action."

"And you think your role is to be part of that revolution?"

"Let's call it a rebel resistance rather than a revolution," I said with a grin. "With my advantages? My education, my financial freedom? How could I not be?"

Judy was quiet for a long moment, watching the trees that had been bare and skeletal when Gunter first called but were now full of summer green. I could see her working through something, weighing whether to voice it.

"You're talking about setting things right," she said finally, her voice carrying a gentleness that somehow made her words more pointed. "But you sound like you're planning to settle scores. Those aren't the same thing, are they?" The question hung between us like the humid morning air. "Keep space for mystery on this pilgrimage," she continued, using the same phrase from months earlier. "For the possibility that you might discover something you're not expecting. Something that changes the questions, not just the answers."

I nodded, though I was already so certain of the direction I was heading that her words felt more like unnecessary caution than wisdom. I had found my cause, my mission, my reason for walking those ancient Italian paths. Francis would understand, I was certain. He had faced the same corrupt institution, the same need for radical action. The only difference was that I wouldn't have to face it alone.

But as I sat there in the morning quiet, Judy's question echoed: Setting things right, or settling scores? The way she phrased it made me wonder if there was a difference. Or rather, the way she said it implied a difference—one that at this point I was not ready to process.

As much as I was encouraged by the Wild Goose experience, it felt unfinished, like the plan was still being worked out. It was exhilarating and unsettling in equal measure—a chorus of wounded believers dismantling the machinery that had harmed them, but not yet sure what could replace it. At the time, I mistook that ferment for chaos. I couldn't yet see that something deeper was trying to be born.

At that point, I did not yet know what Francis's story might offer in bringing my own journey into focus. I sensed that he, too, had lived at a hinge between collapsing certainties and new possibilities, but I couldn't yet see how his life fit into the puzzle. Perhaps that was the unspoken reason I was drawn to Italy—to discover whether his path might reveal a pattern that could hold all these restless pieces together.

Noblesse Oblige

Returning from Wild Goose, stirred up by my discovery of a rebel alliance of progressive brothers and sisters, I threw myself back into my Francis research with renewed intensity. The revolutionary spirit I had encountered at the festival gave new meaning to everything I was learning about the medieval saint. Here was someone who had faced the same choice I was wrestling with—how to respond when the institutional Church becomes the very thing it was meant to oppose.

Over my months of preparation, I learned to use walking sticks, built up the mileage, lost fifteen pounds, and nearly became a Catholic. Not really, but I did fully dispatch my previous evangelical conviction that they were bound for hell. More importantly, the portrait that emerged of Francis and the times in which he lived proved far more compelling than I had anticipated.

This was no quiet, nature-loving caricature from Zeffirelli's "Brother Sun, Sister Moon" that had lingered in my memory since college. Francis was a warrior-poet, a troubadour knight whose spiritual revolution began in the language of a kind of medieval chivalry I could immediately understand. And uncomfortably recognize.

Giovanni di Pietro di Bernardone—the future Saint Francis—was born into thirteenth-century Assisi as the son of a wealthy cloth merchant. His father Pietro had positioned the family among the emerging merchant class that was challenging the old feudal order, and young Francis embodied all the romantic aspirations of his generation. I could almost feel the imported silks and hear the clink of coins in Pietro's strongbox as he counted profits from the finest fabrics in Italy. Francis dressed in these luxurious materials, led the revels of Assisi's youth, and dreamed of achieving knightly glory on distant battlefields.

But Francis wasn't just a rich merchant's son playing at nobility—he was a troubadour in the truest sense. He had fallen in love with the traveling singer-poets who roamed medieval Europe with lutes and lyres, carrying tales of courtly love and chivalric honor from castle to castle. These jongleurs, as they were called, represented everything Francis yearned for: artistic freedom, romantic adventure, and the kind of cultural influence that transcended mere commercial success.

What I was coming to appreciate was that Francis's troubadour training would prove surprisingly important to his later effectiveness as a communicator. Like Bob Dylan in my time, Francis understood that the most powerful performers aren't necessarily the most polished. Francis himself was more like James Taylor: simple, clear storytelling.

He was coming to see what every great poet and songwriter eventually learns: the art is strongest when the artist disappears. At their best they work like windows, not walls—inviting attention beyond themselves. The troubadours we still remember are known less for their personalities than for how they made ancient stories feel immediate and alive.

That said, at fifteen or sixteen, when Francis was taken by this love of the traveling poet-singers, he had no lofty goals—he was still the party boy that loved to own the room when he could. He wrote verses, serenaded the young girls of Assisi, and held the center of attention at every gathering with his musical performances. But his songs weren't just entertainment—they celebrated the very life he longed to live himself. The troubadour tradition celebrated the noble warrior who fought for just causes, who protected the innocent, who transformed the world through valor and virtue. It was the kind of vision of noble adventure that captures the heart of boys just fighting their way into manhood in every generation.

As much as I was drawn to Francis's artistry as a musician and communicator, I was intimidated by his later clarity and boldness. Although, somewhat like Francis, in any new thing I tackled I tended to give it a bear hug, not just a handshake. And now, emerging from Wild Goose, I found myself once again feeling stirred to join a movement, to be a part of something bigger than me. In my naïve and hopeful state, I didn't have any clear sense of what this really meant practically. But it sure seemed like a good headspace for marching through the middle of Italy for three weeks.

I didn't notice it at the time, but what was surfacing was that same bold certainty I had used in fighting my evangelical battles. I had no notion that there might have been something in how I was fighting that contradicted what I was fighting for.

Young Francis's opportunity for glory came in 1202 when Assisi declared war on neighboring Perugia. At twenty, he eagerly enlisted, purchasing the finest armor his father's wealth could provide and riding out with the cavalry as a knight-errant ready to prove his valor. This was his moment—the chance to turn his family's money into real honor through brave fighting.

Was this, in a sense, the medieval version of the way I was stirred up by the Wild Goose experience? The moment when idealism meets opportunity. When someone with resources and privilege finds someone or something in need of rescue. Armed with superior equipment. Convinced that the fight ahead was both righteous and necessary.

I no longer had the excuse of too little time or too little money that I had used successfully for several decades. This reminded me of a term I had learned in college—noblesse oblige. I think it means "nobility obligates." I'm certainly not a noble, but I am one of those fortunate Americans better off than most nobles in Francis' time. Their homes were cold and damp, their clothes were mothy, and they sat on stone latrines.

Francis's chivalric dreams met brutal reality at the Battle of Collestrada. The forces from Assisi were completely routed, and Francis spent a year in a Perugian prison, his romantic notions of glorious warfare shattered by the grim realities of medieval combat and the desperation of a damp, disease-ridden dungeon.

I did not expect trauma or defeat in my quest, as the battle lines were not yet clear to me, nor even the boundaries of the disputed territory. But I did know I was risking neither life nor limb. There would be no swords or imprisonment. While I was drawn to Francis's courage and engagement, what I was heading for was no Battle of Collestrada. There would be no weapons, no blood, and I wasn't even sure exactly what the target was.

When I tried to define what I meant by "the Church is broken," I had only sketchy outlines. Unlike Francis's clear enemy at Perugia, my target seemed to be shifting—was it doctrine? Leadership? Tribalism? Bad theology? All of the above? Maybe that tangle of ideas and feelings was my diseased, damp dungeon.

Francis at least knew when he'd been defeated. How would I even recognize my own Collestrada when I wasn't sure what I was fighting? Could it be that the lesson I was supposed to be taking from this is that while I saw myself as a warrior ready for battle, in reality I was someone who had already lost and didn't even know it yet?

I did not like swimming in such deep water; the cross currents were unpredictable. So I turned back to things I could get my mind around—fun things like what kind of socks to buy and whether my boots were going to be adequately broken in.

I hadn't given enough thought to the practical stuff, apparently. That became painfully clear when the last day before I left arrived and I tried packing three weeks' worth of travel into a single backpack. Having avoided this crucial task until the last minute, I was paralyzed by the gap between what I thought I needed and what I could actually carry.

"This isn't going to work," I said, slightly out of breath from the effort. "I have too many things and too little space."

"Didn't I tell you weeks ago that you needed to focus on traveling light?" Judy gave me this reminder as I stood in our bedroom, staring at a bed piled with far more clothing and gear than any reasonable backpack could contain.

"The story of our rich American lives!" she said, watching my comedy of over-preparation with familiar amusement. "At this point, you just need to lean in and go."

She was right, but I wasn't in the mood to hear it. The packing dilemma had become a metaphor for everything else I was struggling with—the gap between my spiritual ambitions and my actual capacity, between the pilgrim I wanted to be and the anxious, over-equipped tourist I was becoming.

"You need to loosen your grip a bit," she continued. She said it kindly, but I still bristled at the critique. "Maybe you've built up some unrealistic expectations."

I knew that working out what I was going to be able to carry in my backpack would be easier than sorting out the baggage I was carrying in my head—too many directions, too many ideas. Trying to make light of my frustration I said, "If it were weighable, I think the baggage in my head would easily exceed the weight limit for carry-ons."

She smirked and then said, "You're going to Italy for the first time in your life! Whatever else happens, you'll see Florence and Rome. There's enough beauty for a lifetime in those two places." She paused, watching me attempt another unsuccessful assault on the zipper. "I think you've gotten so wound up about your 'deconstruction project' that you might miss something more important."

Of course she was correct. But by reflex I pushed back. "What's more important than getting closure on questions of faith? Isn't that at the heart of everything else?"

But even as I said it, I heard the implied absoluteness—the certainties of my evangelical heritage that were still embedded deep in my bones.

"I hear that," she said patiently. "I just know you well enough to see the risk that you may be walking over hallowed ground and not see it if you're stuck talking to yourself instead of looking and listening."

"Yes, I know. I'll take in the art and the landscape and the history, don't worry."

"Just saying it don't make it so," she replied.

"Yes, yes, I'll pay attention."

Irrespective of my impatient tone, I really did appreciate the importance of what she was telling me. Maybe just not right then.

"So, you're trying to fit all this into that backpack? One backpack? For three weeks?" she asked, scanning the chaotic heap on the bed.

She spotted the two books I'd carefully selected right away. "These need to go on your iPad."

"But I like having actual books—"

"iPad," she said as though the decision had already been made. "Books are heavy and bulky."

Through a process of elimination that felt surprisingly liberating, she helped me sort the have-to-haves from the want-to-haves. Nine shirts became four. Five pairs of pants became two. Two dozen pairs of socks became one dozen. My complaints fell on deaf ears; she was only focused on practicality and efficiency.

When I started moaning about the smaller numbers, she gave me that look. "Remember the art of washing your underwear in the sink that you mastered in college when you were in that apartment with three other guys? Time to bring back some of that knowledge."

About halfway through the process, I realized my CPAP machine was still in the drawer and hadn't been part of my calculations. When we pulled it out and stuffed it into its nonnegotiable space, it took up about twenty-five percent of the pack. Which, of course, meant pulling out even more things.

In the end, it closed. Barely.

As I drifted off to sleep that night, I was able to shuffle all the things that had been concerning me into that box called "think about it later." That required no space in my backpack. I found it helpful to actually picture each concern, name it, picture putting it into the box and closing the lid. One of those silly mental tricks that actually seems to work. I knew I would have eight to ten hours of flight and travel time before the pilgrimage actually began. That should give me time to sort out what was vital and what was not.

The Redshift

I arrived at Raleigh-Durham International Airport two hours early to accommodate the international flight, though the security lines for overnight departures proved nothing like the chaos for earlier flights. Just me and my bulging backpack—everything I thought I'd need for three weeks compressed into overhead bin dimensions.

The first leg to Rome would be eight hours to a connection in Paris. As we climbed through the Carolina night sky, I settled back and tried to gather my thoughts about what exactly I was carrying into this pilgrimage. Wild Goose had turned my personal musings into a quest. I was heading to Italy, not as a confused evangelical refugee, but as someone who had found a new way forward—a more progressive approach to Christianity, one with more coherence and moral clarity.

The more I thought about it, the more I realized this wasn't just about reforming Christianity—it was about a Christianity that took systemic and institutional change seriously. Things like climate change, economic inequality, the way wealth gets concentrated while communities and ecosystems get stripped bare. These weren't just issues of personal salvation—they were existential, requiring a mature faith that could grapple with complexity rather than retreating into simplistic answers.

Francis was simple but he was not simplistic. With bare feet and a threadbare tunic, he pulled off some very sophisticated and strategic things in his dealings with the institutional Catholicism of his time.

It seemed a bit surreal to be hurtling through the air nearly five hundred miles an hour, almost seven miles above the Pyrenees, all to walk in the footsteps of history's most famous poor person. The Pyrenees, the mountain range separating Italy from France, were crossed yearly by young Francis and his father on their annual buying trips to the cloth fairs of Troyes. By caravan and horseback it would take them thirty days for the journey; we would cover that same ground in thirty minutes.

As we reached cruising altitude and the cabin lights dimmed, I could just make out, across the middle seat and through the window of my seatmate, twinkling points of light—stars. We were above the clouds. The hum of the engines had settled into a steady rhythm.

My seatmate was a reserved looking man in his 40s. His age and the Duke logo on his shirt suggested he might be a professor. He had been quietly reading. He closed his book in a deliberate way and turned to gaze out the window, which I thought was odd given that above the cloud cover there really was nothing to see.

"So much darkness," he said softly, almost to himself, "yet each one of those points of light is larger than we could easily comprehend. And all of it—this entire cosmos—nearly fourteen billion years old."

"It's gotten older since the last time I heard that number," I said by way of a light introduction.

He chuckled. "We learn more all the time. The measurements keep getting more precise."

"How do we even know how old the universe is?"

"The Big Bang theory, mostly. When we discovered that the universe was expanding—through redshift measurements—we could work backwards to estimate when it all began." He paused, still gazing out at the stars. "Actually, that discovery was quite controversial when it first emerged."

"The Big Bang controversial? I guess I kind of assumed it was self-evident. I mean, we've been talking about it for a few thousand years—you know, 'In the beginning' and all that."

"Yes, and the controversy initially wasn't among the religious—it was among the scientific community. Due to the bitter overhang of the Enlightenment and its relationship to religion," he said, glancing at me as if to ensure I was still listening, "science had settled on a more static view of the universe, more like they have in the East—massive cycles, everything going around and back again. It suited our skeptical nature better than what many saw, and still see, as superstitions from ancient texts."

"By that do you mean the Bible?" I asked with an unnecessarily curt tone.

I caught myself, surprised by the defensive edge in my voice. I had years ago dropped trying to defend the Bible as trying to make it something that it was never intended to be—I had fully stepped off the pedestal of inerrancy. Yet here I am still able to be provoked.

Giving me a moment to settle, he continued. "Yes, the Bible. And the Quran and many of the texts of the Hindus." He paused. "I should clarify—the problem is not with the texts themselves. They are rich and deep and interesting. The problem is more with those who don't read them for what they are, but for what they want them to be—something revealed and absolute."

Continuing, more calmly now, I agreed. "You know, I have noticed that it's those with the most certain conviction, usually about something absolute, who cause the most trouble.

"And the problem exists on both the left and right." This was an important insight I had not seen in my evangelical Republican days. "It affects both those interested in radical change as well as those defending traditional historical views."

"That's absolutely true!" He paused for a second with a slight smirk to see if I would get the joke.

"Yes, absolutely," I replied.

"I've neglected to introduce myself," he said. "I'm a professor at Duke—astrophysics. Julian Hartman, but you can call me Jules."

"So you're a professional with this star stuff?" I asked.

He chuckled. "Star stuff indeed."

"I'm Jonathan," I said. "Retired and on a quest," I added in a light fashion.

"On a quest? Interesting. What kind of quest?"

"I'm going on a pilgrimage in Florence—the Way of St. Francis. Walking 100+ miles over three weeks through Tuscany and Umbria to Rome."

He nodded politely but seemed distracted.

"Are you stopping in Paris?" I steered back to small talk.

"Actually, I'm meeting a colleague there who works at CERN. We're collaborating on some fascinating particle acceleration experiments."

"CERN—all I know about it is it's like a giant wagon wheel buried underground that's miles in diameter and you try to make things collide. Maybe you can help me—what exactly is CERN?"

"It's the European Organization for Nuclear Research. That's actually not a bad picture of it—the Large Hadron Collider is twenty-seven kilometers around, about seventeen miles, buried underground along the French-Swiss border. We accelerate particles to nearly the speed of light and smash them together. We're essentially trying to understand the fundamental nature of reality by breaking matter down to its most basic components."

"Blowing things up to find out what makes them tick—sounds like something I used to do as a teenager." Then more seriously, "When you say reality, I assume you mean physical reality. The material of the universe?"

"Yes, of course," he said, missing my implication that materiality might not be the only way to think about reality. "We're living through a historically extraordinary period in human understanding of the cosmos. What we're discovering is reshaping much of what we thought we knew about the nature of existence itself."

"The nature of existence itself?" I paused. "That's awfully expansive framing."

Without missing a beat, he continued, "We're probing the quantum realm at energies that recreate conditions from just after the Big Bang. We're finding that reality at the smallest scales behaves in ways that defy common sense."

"Quantum physics—as fundamentally baffling as antimatter and black holes."

He smiled. "Yes, our field has both its angels of light and its demons of darkness."

I took the comment as an oblique nod to my medieval quest.

He paused, gazing out at the stars. "You know, the more we discover about the cosmos, the stranger it becomes. We're finding that reality operates in ways that defy common sense. Particles that exist in multiple states simultaneously, space that's expanding into . . . well, nothing that we can yet comprehend."

I felt myself drawn in despite not understanding half of what he was saying. "It sounds like science is discovering the universe is far more mysterious than we thought." I often said naïve and obvious things like this when I didn't know what else to say.

"Yes, we are. It's something that makes us uncomfortable. Scientists don't like things that they have not yet figured out how to measure or analyze. Fortunately, mysteries—even deep ones like these—tend to go away as the boundary of our knowledge keeps expanding."

After a beat, he shifted to the more personal. "So your quest to Italy—are you moving towards something or away from something?"

It was a particularly perceptive question, and I wasn't sure of an answer. "A little of both, maybe. I'm deconstructing fifty years of evangelical wiring, but I have hope there's something underneath it or behind it or within it that still makes sense."

He nodded thoughtfully. "You know, the old-line evangelicals— what we used to call fundamentalists—initially embraced proof of the Big Bang, but only for part of what it revealed."

"That's interesting. What do you mean?"

"They realized it was proof that the universe had a beginning. After a few hundred years of scientific materialism assuming the universe was static and eternal, most scientists had been leaning against the inherited Judeo-Christian notion of a starting point, a point of creation."

"Yeah, that really is a big deal. I can understand why they'd celebrate that."

"But here's the curious thing—they dropped it after that. They missed what redshift was really telling us: that the universe isn't finished."

"Redshift?" I asked, only vaguely aware of the term.

"Oh yes, sorry. Redshift is the stretching of light waves from objects moving away from us, which makes their light appear redder and tells us the universe is expanding. Measuring the rate of expansion is how we were able to work our way back to the big bang."

As he spoke, my mind wandered to the cosmic distances we'd been discussing. That I had never heard Christian friends, even the "creationists", discussing this was notable. I offered, "What happens after the bang strikes me as more important than the bang itself. Sort of like getting excited about the birth of your child, then leaving the hospital and forgetting them in the nursery."

"Oversimplified, but yeah, that captures it. And although this notion of an open evolving universe might sound radical, it actually fits with what we see every day. It's intuitively true."

I paused. "So they celebrated evidence that the universe had a beginning, but then . . ."

"Exactly. They grabbed the part about the beginning and missed that we're living in an unfinished cosmos—one that's been creating itself for nearly fourteen billion years and is still becoming something more."

"I would've thought they'd embrace that. A living, breathing universe sounds like the God we talk about."

"Precisely. But not the God they said they believed in—unchanging, immutable, fixed, disconnected from this beautiful mess we live in."

"That sounds more like the God of Plato than the messy God of the Hebrews."

"Exactly. And Aristotle. Both ended up with unchanging, perfect divine reality set apart from our changing, material world. That's the philosophical dislocation."

"That reminds me of a C.S. Lewis quote about Plato. It was something to the effect that everything in Western philosophy since Plato is just a footnote on his work."

"C.S. Lewis, the children's author?" Julian asked, then continued, "Yes, I know that quote and it's a great one, but I think it was actually said by Whitehead. Lewis might've been referring to what he said." He said this with the parent-child tone that very smart people sometimes use when correcting others, a little bit condescending.

Moving back to our discussion of the Redshift he said, "This discovery happened at an interesting cultural moment as well. This was at the time when the story of evolution was becoming rooted in other fields, the most controversial of which was public education. When all this discussion about redshift was going on, fundamentalists were still fighting over whether the theory of evolution should even be taught in our public schools. Remember the Scopes monkey trial? That happened in 1925. This was going on at the same time as Hubble was using his telescope to make his redshift observations."

"Yeah, I recently read that even after Scopes was found guilty, it remained illegal to teach evolution in Tennessee schools until 1967."

After pausing for a moment to reflect on just how long change can take, I continued, "This is thinking way outside the box for me."

"Yes, it's tricky. More than thinking outside the box, it's more like asking whether the box is even necessary."

I felt something fundamental shifting inside me. I realized that the crusading mission that had so occupied my focus now seemed like a very small subplot in a much larger story.

Eventually, I tried to sleep, but I kept returning to this notion of an unfinished universe. It struck me how different it would be to start with an unfinished universe still learning and growing, rather than a perfect one we came along to break. The implications felt overwhelming but oddly hopeful—like Job confronted by the whirlwind.

When I finally dozed off, I had a dream that replayed a bungee jumping experience I had decades earlier. I clearly remembered the terror of the moment, standing gripping the edges of a slightly swinging metal cage that the crane had hoisted 180 feet off the ground. The attendant said, "Count to three, I will tap you on the shoulder." When the three count came, it wasn't a tap—it was a shove. In those first interminable seconds of freefall I said the shortest prayer of my life: "Oh Jesus." But the exhilaration as the extending band slowed my descent and began pulling me back in an arc that allowed me for just a moment to pretend I was Superman—it was a beautifully unbounded thing.

"We are now beginning our descent," came the voice from the cabin speakers.

I looked at Jules. "Good luck with your friend and the exploding particles."

He smiled. "Sometimes you can actually learn something from crashing into things at very high speeds."

"If you survive it!" I chuckled.

I wasn't sure exactly how he meant it, but I took it at face value: Discovering new things requires breaking down old ones, and sometimes that breaking down requires a great deal of energy and momentum. I wondered what it might suggest about my pilgrimage.

During our stop in Paris, as passengers deplaned for the city and travelers boarded for Rome, I stepped out into the aisle and wished Julian well. Rather than sit, I decided to walk around a bit. The initial stiffness reminded me of my limits and age, but I also noticed that just a handful of steps down the aisle, with the blood flowing, the pain went away quite quickly. If only the lingering stiffness of my inflamed evangelicalism would dissipate so easily.

The remaining two hour flight went quickly. I was looking forward to getting a more ground-level experience of Francis— the feet in the dirt part rather than the head in the clouds.

When we began our descent into Rome, the night was behind us and looking east I could see the rising sun starting to define the Italian horizon. Soon I would be walking—walking a lot—but now I felt I was ready.

Off the Rails

Although I long ago lost my fear of flying, I still hold my breath in those last moments before you hear the chirp chirp of the wheels when they skip along the tarmac. It's right before the engines abruptly reverse thrust to turn our forward momentum into a crawl. As we landed, we all pitched forward as the plane slowed faster than our bodies wanted to—the lap belt cutting into my gut—a literal gut check.

As I tumbled out of the plane into the terminal at Leonardo da Vinci–Fiumicino airport, the swirl soon humbled my enthusiasm. Fiumicino sprawls in every direction—endless corridors, swarming signage, a steady churn of bodies. I'm easily pulled off course in places like this; the arrows all point somewhere, just not necessarily where I need to go.

The first order of business was finding and getting through customs. That actually went very smoothly. Just stayed with the flow from my plane. On the other side of customs I started to relax a bit. I had plenty of time, so I found a place for a cappuccino and a croissant to plan out the day. I had heard that Italian croissants are similar to French but often softer and sometimes filled with jam, pastry cream or Nutella. Oh, Nutella—I was told I will love it. I doubted I would.

One cappuccino and a forgettable cornetto later, I had burned through the extra time I had. The corridors of Fiumicino's airport stretched in every direction and soon I was lost. Every arrow seemed to confidently point somewhere, but my foggy, travel weary brain felt a little cross-wired. I had one of those episodes—only seconds long—where my thoughts go blank and I worry that my age is catching up with me, that maybe I'm really too old to be doing this. In a moment it passed, and I had complete clarity about the fact that I was a bit lost and didn't know which direction to go.

Wandering around somewhat aimlessly for more time than I should have, I eventually swallowed my pride, turned on Google Translate, and looked for someone who might help. I glanced at my watch and noticed that I had lost track of time. My margin for getting to Florence in time for lunch was dwindling. I should not have stopped for the Nutella-filled croissant. Honestly, why Nutella? It was not unpleasant, but why it was so popular was not at all clear to me.

I spotted someone—not an official, apparently part of the janitorial staff. I blurted out, clearly with impatience, that I was trying to find the train to Florence. I read my Google screen in very slow, over-enunciated Italian: "Dov'è il treno per Firenze?"—"Where's the train to Florence?" He smiled, nodded, and pointed toward a sign just a bit further on the way I was already going.

Here I was, supposedly setting out on a spiritual quest, and I couldn't even navigate an airport without technological assistance and the kindness of strangers. Maybe this was exactly the kind of humility that pilgrimage was supposed to teach—the recognition that I needed guidance, that my plans weren't bulletproof, that getting lost might be part of the point.

Fortunately, once I found the train, I saw that new trains left every half hour or so. I had just missed the last one, so by the time I boarded and was on the way, I had missed my window for the lunch meetup. I texted Gunter, suggesting they go ahead for some sightseeing in Florence and not wait for me—we could meet up at dinner. I actually might like a few hours in Florence to get my bearings before dropping in with my soon-to-be friends.

The door slid closed behind me with a gentle hiss, like a sigh. I stowed my pack, found my seat, and let out a breath I didn't know I was holding. The station had been chaotic, but the train was quiet, almost serene.

As the Italian countryside rolled past my window, I found myself returning to this idea about an unfinished universe. What if creation wasn't a completed project but an ongoing work—something still being written, still being discovered? The thought felt both unsettling and liberating.

If the universe wasn't yet finished, then neither was my story. Perhaps at 68, wandering through Italy with questions I couldn't answer, I wasn't too late for anything.

The train swayed gently as we picked up speed, and I watched olive groves blur into vineyards, then into small towns with red-tiled roofs. Each scene felt like a page turning in some vast, unwritten book. Julian's words echoed: sometimes you learn something from crashing into things at very high speeds. Maybe that was what an unfinished universe required—momentum, collision, the willingness to break apart old certainties to make room for whatever was still being born.

The train had just left Roma Termini and rolled smoothly through the hills of Lazio. I had a window seat, second-class carriage, with a small table between me and a man in his early fifties, intent on a sheaf of papers. The lines on his face suggested someone much older. His navy blazer and rumpled Oxford shirt showed him to be a businessman who traveled a lot. His leather satchel bore an embossed Star of David that had been worn smooth. I wouldn't have noticed if I hadn't reached down for my pen and caught the detail.

"You're American?" he asked, as the train passed a vineyard-lined slope.

"Yes, I am. North Carolina, more specifically. What gave me away?"

"I heard you speaking to the attendant."

"And you?" He had traces of a New York accent mixed in with some other things I could not place.

"Raised in New York, Long Island. But I live in Tel Aviv now. I'm in venture capital, focused on agricultural technology investments. Looking at an investment opportunity in Florence." He continued, "I'm taking a few extra days to visit the galleries. I'm David, by the way. David Feinman."

I introduced myself. The fact that he was a VC meant that we had plenty to chat about given my background in investing. I was on familiar ground talking with venture investors.

Despite their caricature as ruthless, most of the dozens I'd gotten to know were insightful, imaginative people, driven less by greed than by the thrill of building something new. They were valuable to entrepreneurs not simply for capital but for their insights and relationships with other entrepreneurs. They were fantastic cross pollinators. They also had experience looking into the fog of the marketplace and sensing what was coming next.

He asked, "How about you? What is the occasion of your visit to Florence?"

"Meeting some friends, then some hiking in the Apennines. Several towns—I know it includes Assisi and ends in Rome."

"Assisi? Beautiful little place. Still looks medieval. Most people go there because of Francis. What has you heading that way?"

"Actually, it is Francis. My friends and I are doing a nearly three-week pilgrimage called 'The Way of St. Francis.'"

He looked at me curiously. "Pilgrimage? I'm not sure I have the energy for such quests anymore."

After a beat, he asked, "Are you Catholic?"

"Actually, Protestant. Or more correctly, former evangelical, trying to escape the overhang of fundamentalism."

With an easy chuckle, David replied, "Thank you for being so upfront about it. That's not too different from the battles between the Orthodox and Reformed in the Jewish camp."

"Apparently, there are fundamentalists everywhere." I hoped my tone wasn't too light. "I sort of feel like if the fundamentalists—Christian, Jewish, or even Muslims, I guess—would more carefully consider what modern science is teaching us, especially now about human psychology, they might loosen their grip a bit on their old certainties."

He paused, glancing around the train car before leaning slightly forward. "You're assuming they want to learn. But from my experience with the ultra-Orthodox, it's not about lack of information—it's about the psychological need for certainty. They seem almost immune to new knowledge when it threatens accepted tribal norms."

"Yes, I get it. I've lost count of how many headstrong battles I've had with friends who break down over unspoken assumptions rather than the logic of our respective arguments." I paused. "I guess you're saying just teaching someone about their biases does very little to remove those biases. Yes?"

"Neither their biases nor their evil intentions." His voice went flat, and he looked directly at me. "My grandfather had three degrees. He spoke five languages, knew Talmud better than most rabbis. His killers? Many of them were highly educated too—Nazi officers with university degrees, engineers who designed the camps, doctors who conducted experiments. My second cousin's family was gassed at Auschwitz—children aged five and seven. Knowledge does not necessarily bring enlightenment. Sometimes it simply makes evil more powerful and precise."

His phrasing struck me. "Evil that's more powerful and precise." It had a deadly weight to it.

"So that my point is not lost," David said, leaning forward, "that men can conspire to engineer such horror is not the most difficult point here. It's the all-powerful God who does not show up."

I immediately thought of Beckett's *Waiting for Godot*. The god that does not show up. The boundary he was mapping was the lip of that existential precipice that the Holocaust had pushed us toward.

"But I need to press this further," David continued, his voice quieter now but more intense. "Because every time I've had this conversation with religious people, they want to talk about human freedom. Free will. The necessity of real choice. And fine—I'll grant you that. Humans did this. Humans built the camps, operated the gas chambers, looked away while the trains rolled past."

He paused, and something harder came into his eyes.

"But what about my nephew? Born with a genetic disorder so rare they didn't even have a name for it. He lived fourteen months. Every day was suffering—seizures, feeding tubes, surgeries that bought him weeks at best. No Nazi did that to him. No human choice. Just . . . biology. Random mutation. And his parents—good people, faithful people—praying every night to a God who apparently couldn't or wouldn't do anything."

The train rocked gently. Outside, the hills of Lazio rolled past, indifferent and beautiful.

"Or go bigger," David said. "Forget humans entirely. Before we even existed—hundreds of millions of years of animals suffering, dying in agony, species going extinct. Tsunamis drowning thousands of creatures who never did anything to anyone. Parasites that eat their hosts alive from the inside. The whole system seems designed to maximize suffering."

He turned to look at me directly. "So here's my question, Jonathan. Not about Hitler—I can blame Hitler. But who do

I blame for childhood leukemia? For the earthquake that killed a quarter million people in Haiti? For the universe itself being structured so that suffering is woven into the fabric of existence?

"Maybe we're working too hard to solve a problem that cannot be solved," David continued. "We're rejecting the most plausible answer."

"What do you mean?"

"Maybe all of our definitions of God are just elaborate coping mechanisms. Maybe there is no God that we have to redefine here."

He turned to look out the window, his voice trailing off. He was not trying to be provocative. I stared out the window for a moment—it felt as though the train I was on had not only jumped the tracks, but that the tracks themselves had disappeared, and the ground was falling away beneath me.

What could I say? The children gassed at Auschwitz. His nephew seizing in a hospital bed. Two hundred million years of creatures tearing each other apart before humans even arrived to make it worse. If I had any honesty left in me, I had to admit I didn't have an answer. The God I'd been taught about—the one who could do anything, who had a plan for everything—that God had no defense against David's questions. If such a God existed, He was either not all-powerful or not all-loving. Or He simply wasn't there at all.

I didn't have an answer. The honesty of that sat between us like something physical.

"I don't know," I finally said. "I genuinely don't know. But I'm not ready to conclude that the absence of an answer means the absence of God. Maybe it means we've been imagining the wrong kind of God—one who sits outside the system pulling strings, when maybe . . ." I trailed off, not sure where the sentence was going.

"Maybe what?"

"Maybe God is in it somehow. Not above it, controlling it, but inside it. Suffering with it." Even as I said it, I wasn't sure I believed it. It felt like grasping at fog.

David gave me a long look. "That's a beautiful thought, Jonathan. But if your God can't stop a child from dying of cancer—if the best he can do is suffer alongside—I'm not sure that's a God worth worshiping. That's just . . . tragedy with company."

The words landed hard. I had no rebuttal. Whatever faith I was carrying into this pilgrimage would have to be honest enough to hold that question without flinching.

As I looked out at the passing olive groves, I thought about how ancient their roots were. Some of these trees had been here for centuries, a few perhaps since Roman times. I noticed the rhythmic clack of the tracks beneath us—clearly the ground had not fallen away, and we were moving forward on rails that were in fact taking us somewhere.

Neither of us seemed ready to stay in that place any longer. David leaned back in his seat and gave a long exhale as though he had just gotten something off his chest. I let a few beats pass, then gestured toward the report he had been reading. "Is this a company you're investing in? Tell me their story—what do they do?"

His demeanor brightened. "It's an agri-tech company in Tuscany. They're deploying soil moisture sensors and using satellite data to time irrigation precisely. Night pumping to reduce evaporation, targeted fertilizer application. The really powerful part is how we use AI to process all this sensor data—predicting optimal irrigation windows, detecting crop stress before human agronomists would spot it." He became progressively more animated as he described the details of the company's technology. "We've seen twenty percent water savings in pilot fields, with better yields and less chemical runoff.

"If we get this right," David continued, "smallholder farmers won't have to choose between their profit margins and their aquifers. It's practical optimism."

"It seems like overnight AI is everywhere."

"It seems that way, but it's mostly marketing hype," David replied. "Everyone with a smart algorithm is slapping the word AI on their technology. Smarter algorithms and more efficient business processes are all helpful, for sure—sometimes massively so. But this new generative AI—something different is going on."

"I've had that same impression, but I can't quite put my finger on it yet. It's not just the sophisticated pattern recognition—it seems to have its own point of view."

"Yes, it's more than pattern recognition—it goes beyond that," he said, his tone becoming more measured. "What we've discovered in our use of it is that after analyzing decades of agricultural data, it started suggesting irrigation strategies that none of our agronomists had considered—timing sequences that defied conventional wisdom but actually worked better. And it's constantly analyzing live climate data, satellite imagery, soil conditions, recalibrating in real time as conditions change."

After pausing for a moment, he continued to press his point. "It's not just predicting what we already know; it's generating approaches that emerge from patterns across disparate domains that were never practical to correlate before." He gestured toward his papers. "Very sophisticated, and ultimately it's making operations more efficient and profitable, but through insights we never would have discovered on our own."

As he explained this, my mind wandered to other industries I knew better. It was clear such fundamental advances went well beyond the chat conversations I had been thinking about from my own experience.

David paused, then said, "You know what I've come to realize? I think we've crossed a threshold. We now have technology that's...alive."

"With all due respect," I said, "aren't you exaggerating? It's not really alive."

"No, I'm serious. It's alive." There was a mischievous glint in his eye, a slight upturn at the corner of his mouth that suggested he'd played this game before. He knew exactly how it sounded—and he was ready.

"Come on, David. You're saying this software is alive like you and me? That it has feelings? Consciousness?"

"No, no—you're conflating life with consciousness." He lifted a hand, enjoying the moment. "I'm not making grand claims about awareness. That's a much bigger question. I'm talking about something more basic."

"What do you mean—basic?"

"Biology. Think about the simplest textbook case: an amoeba. One cell. No brain. No inner world to speak of. Yet we call it alive because it's an organized system that responds to its environment and keeps adjusting in order to persist."

"And you're saying AI does that?"

"In a limited sense, yes." He leaned forward. "This agricultural AI monitors thousands of signals—soil moisture, temperature, pests, yield data—and it changes its recommendations based on what happens. It learns from each growing season."

He shrugged, satisfied with making his point. "It's not alive the way an organism is—no cells, no metabolism, no beating heart. But it isn't static machinery either. It's adaptive, self-correcting, shaped by experience. Not conscious. Not human." He smiled. "Just technology that learns."

"You know, I've been in the technology industry for twenty-five years, and I can't tell you how many times I've heard something called 'artificial intelligence' when it was really just sophisticated decision trees, better algorithms. But it didn't actually learn. It just followed more complex rules."

"Exactly," David said. "That's what makes this different." He paused, the implications settling in.

I continued, "The ability to actually learn from experience, adapt, improve—that really is the threshold, isn't it?

David nodded. "Most people haven't grasped how fundamental that shift is. We went from tools that process to tools that learn. This change is not just incremental improvement—it's a change of many orders of magnitude.

He looked out the window for a moment, then back at me. "I think for most of us, the moment we knew it had come to life was when our queries became conversations."

That landed perfectly. He was right—that was exactly the shift. Not just asking and receiving, but genuinely conversing, with the AI asking clarifying questions, remembering context, building on previous exchanges.

"When the tool started asking us questions back," I said slowly. "That's when we stopped using it and started engaging with it."

"Precisely," David said. "And once you see that shift, you can't unsee it."

"I'm not from an engineering background, so I really hadn't given much thought to how useful AI could be for something like farming. My interactions have been more around preparing for this pilgrimage—lots of questions about history and theology and philosophy."

"Yeah, that's a different game, but I've played around with some of that also. I get that same sense of AI having its own point of view. It's like the difference between a good assistant and a great one—instead of just going and doing what you've asked them to do, they stop for a moment to consider and suggest alternative courses of action before proceeding. It's a broader and more trusting relationship."

David tapped the cover of the prospectus he had been reading. "I discovered this accidentally in my work, from the need to review proposals like these. I started experimenting with feeding key details about new business opportunities to AI and asking for its analysis. It took only a handful of sessions to realize I was getting clearer thinking than I typically get from the passionate entrepreneurs dropping proposals in my inbox."

"Really? How so?"

"Well, entrepreneurs are usually inflating market projections, minimizing competitive threats, overestimating their capabilities—all the usual ego-driven distortions. After years of filtering through those biases to find the actual insights, I immediately noticed what AI wasn't doing. No overselling, no wishful thinking, no selective metrics to make the opportunity look better. Just clear-eyed analysis. It presents the landscape without needing to be right. No academic turf to defend, no reputation to protect."

"That's been my experience too. With really complicated questions about morality and religious practices and historical quandaries, what I noticed in the answers is they never seem biased, extreme, or contradictory. I wonder why that is?"

"It comes from how they're trained. Have you heard the term 'large language model'?"

"I've heard the term. I know they are what's used to train generative AI chatbots, but I have no real understanding of what they are. Sounds like a master framework for grammar and language. But I know it's much more than that."

"Engineers are not very good at naming things. Case in point is this term 'large language model.' That was an adequate description of what they were doing initially, but now, given the oceans of data that are being digested, it should be called something more like a comprehensive human culture model."

"Yes, you're right—the phrase 'comprehensive human culture model' carries a very different meaning than 'large language model.'"

He continued with the level of detail I would expect from a careful investor. "The large language models used to train AI draw from three primary pools: books, scientific and academic research, and web content. Of the roughly 130 million books that are available throughout the world, roughly 50 million have already been digitized through projects like Google Books and Internet Archive. Similarly, nearly half of the hundred million plus journal articles and scientific research papers available for review have also been digitized and added to the models, with 3-5 million new papers published annually."

"That's all the books and papers—they've also hoovered up all the website content, haven't they?" Having run a web portal company, this is a familiar domain.

"Yes, I neglected to mention the biggest one. Nearly 1.2 billion websites—the web component alone is about five times the size of the books and research papers that are part of the models."

"It sounds like what you're saying is that generative AI gives us a window into what is effectively an encyclopedia of all the wisdom and knowledge of humanity."

"Yes. That's it. The AI doesn't create wisdom from nothing; it finds patterns across this unprecedented collection of human understanding."

"You're saying it's more like a window to something else rather than something in itself?"

"Yes, a window, but a very unique kind of window. It's not just a faster card catalog—it's more like a kaleidoscope. Every time you ask a question, you turn the cylinder and the whole library re-indexes itself around what you're trying to figure out. It appears that when human knowledge is dynamically recombined across domains, previously unseen patterns and insights emerge."

I sat with that for a moment, watching the Italian countryside blur past. The implications seemed significant.

"You know," David said, his investor's mind clicking into gear, "I think most people don't grasp the sheer scale of what's happening right now. The capital flowing into AI—it's orders of magnitude beyond anything we've seen before."

I thought about my own company, riding the first tech wave. "The dot-com era seemed huge at the time."

"It was huge," David said. "Until it wasn't. When the bubble burst, the NASDAQ dropped nearly 80%. Over $5 trillion in market value just evaporated. The market took fifteen years to recover what was lost."

"And that doesn't even count all the private companies, like mine, that never made it into the public market numbers." I wasn't sure of the exact figures, but I knew there were tens of billions raised for companies that never became publicly traded stocks.

"And those founders," David said, "ended up losing their companies. Diluted into oblivion."

"And out of the ashes came Google, Amazon, a reborn Apple—"

"And Nvidia," David finished. He paused. "You know, thirty years ago, Americans genuinely feared Japanese technology would dominate the world. Sony, Toshiba, the semiconductor threat. You remember that anxiety?"

"Oh, absolutely. It was everywhere."

"Well, one single American company—Nvidia—is now worth more than five times Japan's entire technology sector. All 415 companies combined."

Time seemed to stop for a moment. David had a look of uncertainty on his face, like he wasn't sure if what he'd just said was good news or bad news. I took a breath and looked out the window. The rhythmic clacking of the tracks had become steady, almost hypnotic. The trees along the line seemed closer than they were—their details blurred into a wash of green and brown. I wondered whether the AI momentum we were discussing had already reached these kinds of speeds—too fast to see clearly, impossible to stop.

"That's the AI revolution," David said quietly. "Different by orders of magnitude. And we're still in the early innings."

"Having said that—there is an ethical shadow over all of this that really must be addressed."

"What do you mean?"

His tone became more serious. "The first large language models were trained by essentially scraping the internet—pulling in massive amounts of published material, including copyrighted work. Books, articles, creative writing. Most of those authors never consented to having their work become training data."

"That's troubling."

"It is. The courts are still sorting out the legal implications. As someone who evaluates AI companies for investment, I have to think carefully about which ones I back—not just their technology, but their ethical foundations." He tapped his prospectus. "Some companies are trying to build more ethical training approaches, licensing content properly, compensating creators. Others took shortcuts in the rush to market."

"So it's not inherent to the technology itself?"

"No—it's about how recklessly some companies approached the training process. Like the printing press. The technology wasn't the problem, but early printers just started copying whatever they wanted without permission or compensation. Eventually, copyright law emerged to address that. We're in a similar moment now with AI."

"But you're still investing in it?"

"Selectively. I look for companies that are thinking carefully about these issues, not just treating them as legal obstacles to work around. The technology has profound potential—but that doesn't excuse ignoring the rights of the people whose life's work went into training these systems."

I nodded, appreciating his thoughtfulness. It was a reminder that even transformative technology carries ethical complexity. The conversation shifted after that, but the point had been made—this window into human knowledge came with real costs to real people, and those costs deserved serious attention.

"You know," he said slowly, "as an investor, I'm used to human advice being compromised. People have agendas, biases, defensive patterns. Financial analysts inflate projections to close deals. Executives downplay risks to maintain stock prices. Even researchers can slant findings to support their theories." He gestured toward his investment papers. "I spend half my time separating signal from noise, trying to figure out what people actually know versus what they want me to believe."

I had seen the same pattern over the course of my career.

"That's why the investment industry is so sensitive about people pitching their own book of investments—why investment positions have to be disclosed. It helps investors adjust for bias."

"Exactly, right. I forgot you know this business I'm in. But back to my point—maybe when you access human wisdom without those defensive filters—no reputation to protect, no position to defend—you discover something different."

He looked out the window, then back at me. "An accidentally egoless intelligence, maybe?"

"Accidentally egoless intelligence"—it's a phrase that seems too important to lay down but too big to defend.

"I don't know, maybe that's overstated. It's just something I've been thinking about." He paused, watching the countryside blur past. "You know, there's this thing psychologists call cognitive switching, which is a very important skill set for someone in my line of business."

"Cognitive switching sounds like just changing your mind," I said with a grin.

"Well, it certainly can often result in that, but really what it is, is the ability to shift perspectives quickly—to see how the same evidence can support different frameworks depending on which lens you're using. Entrepreneurs who can't do that, who get too attached to their original assumptions or trapped by their investment in one approach, miss what the evidence is actually telling them."

"I can see that. The investors in my company wanted me to be confident and enthusiastic but were wary of me overselling the vision."

The train slowed as we approached Florence. An overhead voice spilled Italian syllables like water over stone. David tucked his papers back into his leather bag, and something in his expression had changed. The confident dismissal was gone, replaced by something more curious, more open.

As the train came to a stop and we stood to gather our things, David said, "I hope your pilgrimage gives you what you're looking for."

"Right now, I'm just focused on getting to the starting point. How the trek unfolds is in God's hands."

He gave me a knowing look, reached out to shake my hand and said, "Yes, perhaps it is in God's hands, whomever or whatever he or she might be."

"Indeed, the categories fail us!" I said. "And good luck with your AI farming venture."

"I prefer insight to good luck, but thank you"

Before releasing his grip, he added quietly, "I hope you find what you're looking for, Jonathan. But be careful—don't settle for answers that work only when you're looking at the easy cases. Those Sunday school answers are of use only to children."

I held his gaze. "I won't. That much I can promise."

He nodded once, a gesture that felt like respect even if not agreement. "Safe travels."

"And for you as well," I replied before releasing his grip.

As I shouldered my pack and made my way from the platform toward the terminal, I felt strangely lighter—unsettled, yes, but no longer crushed by the need to defend a system I could no longer make sense of. It was as if some invisible burden of proof had slipped from my shoulders, even though I couldn't yet explain why. From all I'd read about the saint we were about to walk behind, his journey seemed to begin in a similar place: not with clarity, but with a stubborn refusal to pretend the old answers still worked.

But David's question didn't fade as I walked through the station. *If your God can't stop a child from dying of cancer, I'm not sure that's a God worth worshiping.* He'd meant "tragedy with company" as a dismissal—a God who can only suffer alongside us is no God at all. But the phrase landed differently for me. I've sat with people in grief. I've been the one grieving. And I know this much: tragedy with company is a different thing entirely than tragedy alone. I couldn't yet say what that meant for God, or for the questions David had raised. But it felt like an ember I wasn't ready to let go out.

Act II: From Proposition to Presence

"My speech and my message were not in plausible words of wisdom, but in demonstration of the Spirit and of power, so that your faith might not rest in the wisdom of men but in the power of God."

—1 Corinthians 2:4-5

"We do not think ourselves into new ways of living, we live ourselves into new ways of thinking."

—Richard Rohr

Breaking Bread

As I exited the train station to look for the taxi stand, I caught my first breath of open air since leaving home. It was a beautiful spring day, and in the breeze, I smelled fresh panini wafting from a nearby sandwich shop. The scene called up an unexpected sense of hope. It felt like my pilgrimage was finally beginning—viscerally, not just philosophically. It was a welcome uplift, good medicine for the disoriented funk I had felt just twenty minutes earlier.

The conversations from my journey had left me carrying questions that felt too big for any containers I had brought to hold them. As uncomfortable as that felt, maybe that's exactly where I needed to be. Yet in this Florentine spring's bright midday light, I wondered whether these larger questions might actually help me focus on what mattered, letting other burdens fall away. If they were true, then their loss meant I might be moving closer to what actually exists rather than what I was taught to believe.

I'd have to think about that more. For now, it was time to turn my attention to meeting up with my friends.

I finally made it to the hotel nearly three hours later than planned. Gunter had arranged our lodgings, and he chose well.

The Hotel Silla is a charming boutique hotel in Florence's Oltrarno district—quieter than the tourist-heavy areas. It sits right on the Arno River and within easy walking distance of the city's landmarks. The Ponte Vecchio was just blocks away, with the famous Duomo Cathedral and the Medici Palace less than a mile away.

As I entered the hotel, the scent of blooming jasmine drifted through the courtyard—sweet, insistent, Mediterranean. I noticed a small piazza beside the hotel, a perfect spot to sip a cappuccino and make notes in my journal.

After checking in, I texted Gunter to tell him I had arrived. Once I got to my room, the travel weariness hit me. After traveling all night, I had that tired, edgy feeling that might make it challenging to get to sleep, but I would be a much better companion at dinner if I could get thirty minutes or so. I fell asleep quickly and didn't wake for over an hour—the kind of deep afternoon sleep that leaves you momentarily disoriented, unsure of where you are or how you got there.

The guitar ringtone of my iPhone woke me up. It was Gunter.

"Hey, stranger, good trip? Are you settling in?"

"The hotel is great, and the location is good." I stifled a yawn as I spoke. "I was able to get a good nap, so I am ready to meet up."

"It sounds like you haven't quite woken up yet," he teased.

"Hey, remember you're on Central European Time, the same time zone you all live in. I crossed six zones to get here. I am due a bit of slack for the next few days."

"Yes, I know, old friend. I'm just teasing. We got here before noon and are on a short walkabout of the city. We should be back and ready for dinner in a couple of hours. We have a reservation at a nice trattoria for eight o'clock; it's a lovely place recommended by the front desk just two blocks from the hotel." I was glad to know I would have a few hours to explore before we met up.

"Sounds good." In his German-accented English, his 'good' sounded like 'goot'. "I am looking forward to meeting Wilhelm and Thomas. Do I recall correctly that you have known these guys since college?"

"Yes, very old friends. We met at university but lost touch as we got older. This is a bit of a reunion for us." He added, "It seems we have grown in very different directions over the intervening fifty years."

"Interesting. That should make for some fun conversations," I said. "I want to go for a short walk, so I'll meet you at the restaurant. Just text me the address."

"Auf Wiedersehen," he said. "See you at dinner."

"Can't wait."

I walked down to the Arno, just a block from the hotel. Reaching the riverbank, I watched the current flow—visible but not swift, more meditative than forceful. This place carried such historical weight. Maybe Florence was the perfect place to find a new orientation. It was the birthplace of the Renaissance, where the iron grip of Catholic orthodoxy first began to loosen.

With its art, science, and daring thought, Florence was a seedbed for a revolutionary way of understanding that prized individual insight over inherited wisdom and empirical discovery over received doctrine. Machiavelli had walked these streets, crafting his unflinching analysis of political power.

Galileo, too, had lived and worked here—and been con-demned here, exiled to house arrest in his villa just outside the city for the audacity of suggesting the earth revolved around the sun. From where we stand now, that seems almost incomprehensible.

I headed back to the hotel as the light began to turn golden. I had time to record a few notes in my journal before dinner, and I wondered what kind of company these fellow pilgrims would be. Would they come carrying certainty or questions like mine? Part of me hoped to find companions who would help me think more clearly. But another part feared being thrust into theolog-ical debates I no longer had the energy to fight. What I needed was not another proving ground but a table where differences could be aired without judgment.

I got ready quickly but got caught up in my note-taking and arrived ten minutes late to dinner. I spotted them right away; they had chosen a table outside, caught up in animated conversation with an open bottle of Chianti and three half-full glasses.

Gunter spotted me first, his face breaking into a broad grin. "There he is! The wandering American!" He rose to greet me with a handshake and a hug, waving me toward the table like I was just in time for something important.

Wilhelm stood as well, pulling out the empty chair. "Please," he said with a slight bow. The gesture was formal but genuine— Old World courtesy that caught me off guard.

As I found my place, the waitress returned with a platter of antipasti and a bread basket. "What can I get you to drink?" she asked.

"If these gents are willing to share their wine, then all we need is another glass."

Gunter picked up the conversation as she departed. "Jonathan! I'm so glad you made it. When we met fifteen years ago, I would have never guessed we might meet in Italy someday for a spiritual pilgrimage."

"Nor would I have," I said. "When I got your invitation last year, I was surprised. All of our conversations over the years have been about politics and rock and roll. I didn't know you had an interest in matters of the spirit."

He replied softly, "We Germans tend to hold such things pretty privately." Then, with a nervous laugh, he added, "Now, we'll have our chance to open all that up."

Gesturing toward the others, he said, "Please meet my friends. This is Wilhelm, or Will if you prefer"—he nodded to a man with nearly rigid posture and a lined, weary face. "A very successful attorney and stickler for facts."

Wilhelm raised an eyebrow with a dry smile. "Gunter, you are too generous." Then, turning to me, "I like to say that I am successful enough to have learned to be suspect of anyone who exaggerates."

Wilhelm had a careful, methodical way about him that I couldn't quite read yet. Only later would I learn how he anchored every theological discussion with "according to scripture"—not aggressively, just matter-of-factly, as though grounding his thoughts in something solid.

"Let's just say he rarely loses a case," Gunter quipped. "As applies to our pilgrimage here, Will is a member of the German

Evangelical Alliance who thinks 'Sola Scriptura' could save the Church from itself." He winked at Wilhelm.

Wilhelm grinned, raising his glass. "It couldn't hurt to try." But I caught a note of defensiveness in his voice, as if he were protecting something precious but fragile.

"And this is Thomas," Gunter continued. "A defender of saints and sacrament."

Thomas winced at the description. "Let's just say I trust the accumulated wisdom of the Church more than our own personal interpretations. Someone's got to remind us we didn't invent this faith yesterday." He paused, his voice taking on a more personal tone. "I remember the moment in my first Mass as a child when the priest elevated the host—something about that mystery, that sense of God becoming present through the community's faith, still anchors me."

As Thomas spoke, I could see the Catholic confidence in tradition and mystery, the sacramental vision that saw God working through the Church's accumulated wisdom. But there was also something guarded in his manner, as if he knew his defense of Catholic authority would be challenged and he was already preparing his responses.

"I'm also a Jungian psychoanalyst and a believer in the power of unconscious wisdom," he added.

A comfortable pause settled over the table. Gunter raised his glass. "To new beginnings and old souls."

"Old friends, new paths," Wilhelm added, lifting his glass.

We clinked glasses all around, and I felt the warmth of being included in something that had clearly been years in the making.

Gunter set down his glass with a contented sigh. "You know what I'm hoping for on this walk? To feel that connection with God again—the kind I had when I was younger. That sense of wonder, of mystery, like God was actually present and surprising. Not just ideas about God, but . . . something alive. Something real." He looked almost embarrassed by his own earnestness. "I know that probably sounds naive."

The moment lingered, then Wilhelm set down his glass with deliberate care. "As long as we're being open, I should be honest about something." He looked at each of us in turn. "I have . . . reservations about all this."

Gunter's expression shifted to curiosity. "About the pilgrimage?"

"About the mystical side of Christianity—contemplation, mindfulness, feeling our way toward truth." Wilhelm's voice was measured but firm. "It feels undisciplined to me. Soft. My Lutheran tradition values order, doctrine, clear boundaries. Scripture. For me, mindfulness is about getting your story straight and making sure your logic is sound."

Thomas grinned. "I think you have the wrong idea about mindfulness. Don't worry—by the time our journey is over, I'll have you doing yoga with me in the mornings."

"Not a chance," Wilhelm replied with a smirk.

The tension broke slightly. Wilhelm continued, more seriously now, "Gunter has been inviting me on this for two years. I finally said yes, but only because of our friendship." He glanced at Gunter with genuine affection. "Otherwise, I would have dismissed this entirely. Walking through Italy chasing some medieval saint's ghost? Looking for spiritual experiences? That's not how faith works in my tradition."

"So why did you come?" I asked, genuinely curious.

"Because Gunter is persistent." Wilhelm allowed himself a small smile. "And because I'm old enough to know that sometimes friendship requires showing up even when you're skeptical. But I want you all to know—I'm not here looking for mystical experiences or spiritual emergence or whatever we're supposed to find. I'm here because my friend asked me to walk with him."

The table was quiet for a moment. The waitress approached with menus, sensing the shift in mood, then retreated.

"Actually," I said slowly, "I appreciate that. More than you know."

Wilhelm looked at me with mild surprise.

"I mean it. I wouldn't have considered this without Gunter either." I picked up my wine glass, studying the way light moved through it. "I went to this festival last year—Wild Goose." I paused for a moment to figure out exactly how to describe this beautiful but odd event.

Before I could continue, Gunter said, "Jonathan, I did not know you were a hunter. Is hunting geese considered a spiritual practice in America?" His expression made it clear he was joking.

I laughed despite myself. "Forgive me, yes, it's an odd name. But what it actually is—it's a gathering for progressive Christians and people deconstructing their faith. Workshops with titles like 'Raising Hell: How Dante Got It Wrong' and 'White Jesus, Black Christ' and 'Eve's Revenge: Biblical Feminism.' It was exhilarating. All these ideas I'd never heard in my evangelical world."

"Ah, the wild goose," Thomas said, recognition in his voice. "The Celtic symbol for the Holy Spirit—unpredictable, untameable. Versus the domesticated dove."

"Exactly," I said. "But here's the thing. All that excitement—was I just looking for a new team to join? A new set of talking points? I spent thirty years as a soldier for one version of Christianity, and I got pretty good at winning arguments. The last thing I want is to become a soldier for a different battle, just with better vocabulary."

"At least the progressive boxes have room to breathe," Thomas offered gently.

"Maybe. But I appreciate Will's honesty about his skepticism. Some skepticism is good and useful—keeps you grounded. Too much and the cynicism bleeds in and you've ruined the project." I looked at Will. "At least you know what you believe and why."

Wilhelm shook his head. "Don't mistake rigidity for clarity. I defend Scripture because the alternative is unworkable—everyone deciding for themselves what's true, what's real. That way lies chaos."

"Or freedom," Thomas murmured.

"Or chaos disguised as freedom," Wilhelm countered.

Sensing some tension between these old friends, I weighed in with my story. "I was part of the Jesus People movement back in the day," I said. "Felt like we were going to change everything."

"Ah, the seventies," Gunter said with a nostalgic smile. "I remember them fondly. Though by the time we were old enough to join the protests in Germany, we were just catching the tail end of the parade."

"Before my time, remember you guys are older than me," Wilhelm said.

"Not that much older," Gunter replied with a grin.

Thomas's voice took on a reflective tone, almost as if reciting poetry: "Better bring your own redemption when you come to the barricades of heaven where I'm from."

"Jackson Browne?" I said, recognizing it immediately. "I love his music. 'The Barricades of Heaven' is about the barrios of Los Angeles where he grew up—these neighborhoods that were both barriers and gateways. He wrote it looking back at being sixteen, running around California trying to hear his own song. That tension between yearning and obstacle."

"The yearning feels authentic because he came up seeing that poverty firsthand," Thomas said. "Not romanticizing it, just witnessing it."

"A troubadour," I said. "He and Francis would have gotten along well."

Wilhelm looked skeptical. "But what does that even mean? It seems contradictory, even obscure."

Thomas smiled gently. "I'm not sure I can define it, Wilhelm. But I know it's beautiful."

"Speaking of beauty, gents," Gunter said, raising his glass, "here we are in Florence—ground zero for a good share of all the beauty created in the Renaissance."

"Well," Gunter said, picking up a menu, "we're certainly not holding back, are we? Good. Let's order something to eat and continue. The antipasti here is supposed to be excellent."

The table grew lively with the clink of glasses and the aroma of good food. The antipasti—olives, cured meats, and chunks of aged cheese arranged on a wooden board—were warmly welcome.

I took a bite of bread, chewing slowly, waiting for flavor that never came. "This bread has no salt. It's kind of tasteless."

"Yes, it's intentional," Gunter said. "Both here in Tuscany and in Umbria, where we'll be spending most of our trek, they don't use salt."

Wilhelm shook his head. "It's our first meal, and I'm already missing proper German bread."

"Why?" I asked. "They must know how bland the bread is."

"There's quite a story behind it," Gunter said. "Goes back to medieval times when salt was heavily taxed. Florence and Pisa were rivals, and the Pisans controlled the salt trade from the coast. So the Florentines said, 'Fine, we'll make bread without your expensive salt.'"

"And they just . . . never went back?" Thomas asked.

"Exactly. Even when the taxes ended, the tradition stuck. They even call it 'pane sciocco'—'foolish bread.' But they say it with affection, like an old joke everyone agrees on. Now they claim their food is so flavorful it doesn't need salty bread competing with it."

"It's because they don't make it to be eaten alone," Gunter continued. "They expect you'll eat it with salty meats and cheeses, with olive oil and wine. It's designed for community."

"They're thinking about the whole, not just the parts," Thomas observed.

As I chewed the unsalted bread with prosciutto, each of us seemed to be carrying our own questions, our own uncertainties.

"You know what this reminds me of?" Thomas said, holding up his piece of bread. "Jonathan, think about it this way—Wilhelm's emphasis on Scripture, it's like this bread. Complete, but . . ." He took a bite of plain bread and made a face. "You need the salt, the meat. Scripture needs the spice of the Holy Spirit."

"Exactly!" Gunter chimed in. "The boring bread is just boring bread. I add the salt of the Spirit—that's what brings it to life."

Wilhelm raised an eyebrow. "Are you suggesting Scripture is boring without your personal interpretation of what the Spirit is saying?"

"It's an interesting take," I said. "But back to the bread itself, I don't think it would go over in America."

"Nor in Germany," Wilhelm agreed. "In Germany we take our bread very seriously. We have over three hundred varieties—rye, spelt, whole grain, pumpernickel, each made from different types of flour."

"And I assume they all have salt?" I asked.

Wilhelm nodded with a slight smile. "Of course they do. Tasteless bread is just for Italians."

Wilhelm took another bite, chewing thoughtfully. "I suppose when you put it with this prosciutto . . . it's not terrible."

"It's growing on me," I admitted. "Though I still think most Americans would find this pretty strange."

As our main courses arrived, Wilhelm turned to me. "So, Jonathan, what is it you do back in America?"

"Recently retired after selling a cloud technology company. Started it during the dot-com boom about 25 years ago."

"Technology," Thomas mused. "That must give you an interesting perspective on all this AI hysteria."

"Is it hysteria?" I asked. "Or legitimate fear?"

"Good point," said Gunter. "But I would add greed as well as fear. Remember, although they're fewer in number, there's also a big group that sees it as amazingly useful for automating all kinds of routine work. Many of them are far more focused on the additional profit than on what the human cost might be for those who've been made redundant."

"Actually, I just had a fascinating conversation about it on the train," I said. "A venture capitalist who invests in agricultural AI. He made this provocative claim that it's already alive—not conscious, just alive in the biological sense. Learning from its environment."

"Alive?" Wilhelm said skeptically.

"That's what I said. But he meant it in the basic sense—like how an amoeba is alive because it learns and adapts. Nothing more dramatic than that." I paused, remembering David's mischievous smile. "Though he did say something that stuck with me—that for most of us, the moment we knew it had come to life was when our queries became conversations."

Thomas leaned forward with interest. "That's exactly what I've been noticing. It's not just answering questions anymore—it's having actual conversations. People are even using it for counseling."

"How do you feel about that?" Wilhelm asked.

Thomas paused. "I'm ambivalent. It helps people who can't find or afford a counselor, which is good. But there's something unsettling about therapeutic relationships with something that has no experience of human suffering."

Wilhelm nodded. "We're having serious discussions about how it's going to change law practice. It might make senior partners more productive, but we won't need as many junior associates anymore."

I set down my wine glass. "It's reshaping every industry it touches. The difference now is that it actually learns—not just following rules like the old systems."

"Gentlemen," Gunter interjected with mock seriousness, "this is too heavy for our first dinner. I suggest we shift to more pleasant matters—like deciding what we want for dessert."

"Good idea," Wilhelm said. "I'll go with what I always get—tiramisu. They really do make it better here than anywhere else."

"It's got to be gelato for me," Gunter chimed in. "I noticed on the menu they have quite a list of flavors. Maybe I'll try a new one."

"They all sound good to me," I said.

As the conversation shifted to lighter matters, I caught Thomas glancing at me with what looked like curiosity. The AI question had been planted but not explored—a seed that would have to wait for better soil.

As the evening progressed, I could sense we were all being careful with each other. There was something guarded in how we talked about our different traditions, as if each of us was protecting something we weren't ready to examine too closely.

"So, Jonathan," Wilhelm said as dessert arrived, "Gunter tells me you were a little hesitant about coming on this trip?"

I laughed. "Well, as you can tell by looking at me, I'm not exactly built for climbing mountains." I raised my glass and tipped it toward them. "But I'm fascinated by Saint Francis, so I'm willing to endure wherever this journey might lead us."

Wilhelm's expression softened slightly. "And what exactly are you hoping to find?"

Thomas raised a hand gently. "Will, let's not get ahead of ourselves. We've just met the man. I don't think we've even addressed that question between you, Gunter, and I yet."

Wilhelm looked embarrassed. "Sorry. Getting ahead of myself." Thomas gave him a nod and a smile that suggested they'd had some prior discussion about ground rules.

"No, no, it's okay," I said. "I like to play with an open hand. I guess you could say I'm trying to figure out how to get beyond a very narrow conservative upbringing. I was raised something of a fundamentalist, and I no longer know what I am—but it's a world away from the simplicity and narrowness of how I was raised. According to the rules of my former tribe, I'm now officially a heretic."

Gunter raised an eyebrow with a slight smirk. "I guess Catholics aren't the only ones to brand their heretics," he said with a chuckle.

Thomas looked slightly annoyed. "It's been centuries since Catholics persecuted heretics. Let's not confuse old stories with where things are now. We now know that chasing heresy is something common to all very conservative fundamentalist approaches—Protestant, Catholic, or Muslim, even among Hindus and Buddhists."

Wilhelm sat quietly through this exchange, but I could see him processing the conversation carefully. Finally, he spoke up. "Just because we no longer label people heretics doesn't mean there are no rules or standards. We can push back against extremes without giving up on the importance of guarding the boundaries of doctrine."

Thomas gave him a slightly exasperated look. "Will, let's not bring up that thorny old conversation just now. I'm really enjoying our dinner."

Wilhelm took the request in good spirits, and the conversation continued on a more polite path. Over the course of our dinner, I noticed what I thought might be a pattern—each of us seeming to test the waters, trying to understand where the others stood without revealing too much of our own vulnerabilities.

We were halfway through our second bottle of exceptionally good cheap wine when Thomas said, "Now that we've loosened up a bit, I'd like to learn more about you guys. What were you thinking about when you made the decision to come?"

Gunter said, "Always the counselor, eh, Thomas?"

"He can't help it," Wilhelm quipped. He then carefully set down his glass, realigned the silverware beside his plate. "My grandmother. Munich. 1943. Three Jewish families in our cellar." He paused, jaw tightening. "Two years. She never talked about God's will. She said: 'You see someone drowning, you throw them a rope.' That's all." Another pause. "Forty years in the Lutheran church. Never found faith that clear again."

Thomas nodded slowly. "I had a client once—successful businessman, good Catholic family. Came to me because he couldn't pray anymore. Turned out his son had committed suicide, and his priest told him the boy was in hell. No exceptions, no mercy. This man had built his whole life on the Church's teachings, and suddenly those same teachings were torturing him." Thomas's voice grew quiet. "Watching his faith crack open . . . it cracked something in me too. Made me realize how much of what we call doctrine is really just our attempt to control mystery."

Gunter leaned back, considering his words. "I spent ten years in a charismatic church. Speaking in tongues, prophecies, healing services—the full program. It was . . . compelling. Like tapping into something beyond ordinary experience." He shrugged. "Then the pastor had an affair, the church split, and suddenly everyone had a word from God about who was right. All that supernatural authority, but nobody could manage basic integrity. I didn't leave because I stopped believing in spiritual gifts. I left because I saw how easily they become tools for control."

They looked at me expectantly. "The Jesus Movement," I said finally. "1972. I was seventeen. We really thought we were going to transform Christianity—barefoot services on the beach, guitars instead of organs, love instead of law.

"One Sunday morning I helped baptize thirty people in the Gulf of Mexico." In my memory I could still taste the salt water. "But by the time I was forty, we'd changed the music and relaxed the dress code, but we were back to baptizing in a tank behind the pulpit and we'd become the very thing we'd rebelled against—comfortable, respectable, asking no hard questions."

Thomas said, "Well, you're asking hard questions now."

"Hopefully not too hard," I said.

Wilhelm's response was immediate and flat. "Every reform becomes the next orthodoxy. It's inevitable."

"Maybe," Thomas said carefully, "or maybe we just haven't figured out how to stay fluid yet."

"Fluid." Wilhelm repeated the word like he was testing its weight. "My wife used that word. Before she left."

The sudden personal revelation hung in the air. Gunter smoothly refilled our glasses, giving Wilhelm space to either continue or retreat. He chose retreat, returning to his bread with methodical precision.

As our server dropped off the check and topped off our glasses with the last of the Chianti in our carafe, I was feeling that very pleasant glow of good fellowship. The joke is that it's the wine talking, but I knew it was more than that. Gunter raised his glass for a final toast and said, "To tomorrow. Our first real day on the trail. We'll finally be walking where he walked."

The four of us raised our glasses as Thomas said, "To the journey." Wilhelm, the one who would always press for more detail, said to Gunter, "So tell us, Herr tour director, what is on our agenda for tomorrow?"

With the poise of the senior VP of HR that he used to be, Gunter began with measured enthusiasm, "We start with the Ponte Vecchio—the main bridge over the Arno for most of Florence's history, a bridge that Francis and others would have crossed every day. It was just simple wood then, not the temple of bling that crowds the bridge now. Then we go to Giotto's bell tower—the most elegant tower in Italy, designed by a painter rather than a sculptor or an architect."

"Painters are very important to this city, aren't they?" I chimed in.

"Many would consider that point self-evident," Wilhelm said. He was probably unaware of how dismissive that sounded.

"Yes, indeed!" Gunter responded. "That's why we'll be ending the day at the Uffizi. There we'll find Leonardo and Michelangelo, Giotto and Raphael, Botticelli—the pantheon of Renaissance masters all under one roof. It's the greatest concentration of artistic genius in the world." He said this the same way he might've given an upbeat speech to his staff back in the day.

"But before the Uffizi, of course, we'll visit the Duomo—Brunelleschi's impossible dome that shouldn't exist by any law of engineering. It was the largest dome in the world for over four centuries, built without any supporting framework while construction was happening. Considered impossible at the time."

It seemed we were ready to loosen our grip on the theological positions we packed for the trip and discover what this pilgrimage might teach us through experience rather than argument.

I found myself caught up in his enthusiasm. There was a sense of relief in thinking about practical things—where we would go and what we would do—instead of trying to figure out how the foundations of the world were laid.

As we walked back to the hotel through the narrow Florentine streets, I realized we'd be getting back at a decent hour.

Back at the hotel, Gunter suggested we share a nightcap.

"This is Italy," he said with a grin. "The bar will be open until the last guest leaves."

We found the hotel bar—really just a small lounge with a handful of tables tucked into what might have once been a sitting room. The bartender, a young woman polishing glasses, brightened when she saw us and gestured toward the corner table.

"Can I get you gentlemen anything?" she asked.

Gunter glanced at us. "Amaro? It's traditional after a heavy meal."

We nodded, and she returned with four small glasses of the dark, bittersweet liqueur along with small bowls of chips and nuts—the Italian ritual of always offering something along with drinks. The first sip was a shock of bitterness. We settled into worn leather chairs that appeared to be as old as we were.

We sat in companionable quiet for a few moments, that pleasant exhaustion that follows good food and better conversation.

Wilhelm surprised us by speaking first. "My wife left me five years ago. Said I'd become a stranger living by spreadsheets and schedules. I came here thinking Francis might teach me . . . flexibility, I suppose." He took a sip of our bitter tonic. "Maybe I just wanted to prove I could still surprise myself."

"I know that feeling," Thomas said quietly. "Thirty years of giving counsel, and I often hear myself saying the same things I've said a hundred times. Wondering if I was missing something."

Gunter nodded. "I hear you. Here I am, just retired, no longer worried about money—and yet I worry. Struggling a bit to find a sense of purpose."

The honesty shifted something between us. Not comfortable exactly, but real—the beginning of trust among men who'd forgotten how to be vulnerable.

Later, lying in bed, I thought about the four of us—broken, searching, but willing to walk together. It was enough to let me sleep.

The Dissipation of the Muses

The next morning, I sat at breakfast with heavy eyes. My attention lagged just behind the moment. We met early, around 7:30. My body showed up, but something in me was still circling, waiting to land. It had been a yawning, restless night—dreams of empty cathedrals and arguments with Julian that ended with me shouting at mathematical equations. I hoped it wouldn't take too many days to catch up on sleep. At a glance, it was clear my companions were not in the same fog.

I knew I was still connected to God, however I might be defining Him. Fifty years of sermons, studies, worship experiences—they'd given me something real, moments of genuine encounter and presence. In my deconstruction I'd already knocked down the non-load bearing walls—the theological claims that contradicted what we know about human development and consciousness, that made God smaller rather than larger, that made the biblical writers into stenographers rather than witnesses. That demolition work was mostly behind me. What remained were the deeper, structural questions—the load bearing walls that hold everything else up. Questions about God's power and human suffering. Questions about whether divine presence meant divine control. The connection to God was real. Rebuilding a coherent framework around it—that was proving harder than I'd imagined.

I'd heard that great beauty could provide what rational argument couldn't—direct transcendent experience uncluttered with arguments. Florence, with the Medicis' patronage, had been a magnet for the greatest Renaissance artists. This pull toward beauty was the heartbeat at the center of the church's tradition of liturgy and music. To this day, I'll often find myself by midweek still replaying the chorus of a song I sang on Sunday, long after I've forgotten what the sermon was about. Maybe here, given time in the presence of such artistic genius, I could learn to dance without the old choreography—improvise rather than follow steps I no longer believed in.

As we walked the few short blocks to the Arno, the city was beginning to stir. It was Saturday, and the day-trippers would soon start arriving—pouring in from Pisa, Milan, and Rome. A half mile up the river, we reached Ponte Vecchio from the quieter south bank. As we had hoped, the bridge was nearly empty.

As we stepped onto the bridge, Gunter lifted a hand as if greeting an audience. "Because of its age and historical importance," he said, pausing for effect, "Hitler himself ordered the bridge spared. This is the only bridge in Florence that survived the bombing during the Second World War."

Wilhelm's expression shifted—something crossing his face too quickly to read. "My grandfather was here," he said quietly. "Wehrmacht. Part of the retreat north in '44." He touched the stone railing. "He never talked about it. Not once."

Gunter glanced at him. "Wilhelm, I've known you for years. You've never mentioned that."

Wilhelm kept his hand on the stone. "Some things are difficult to talk about."

The silence held for a moment.

Sensing Wilhelm would appreciate turning our attention to something less personal, I asked, "So Francis would have crossed the older one?"

Thomas nodded. "Francis used the bridge about a century earlier. When he crossed, it was just a narrow footbridge. Simple, functional. No shops."

Wilhelm, after a moment, gestured at the glittering displays with what looked almost like embarrassment. "Nothing like . . . this excess."

I glanced around at the high-end displays—gold jewelry, luxury watches. "What would Francis have thought of all this?"

The morning light caught the facets of a cut stone in one of the rings, sending small rainbows reflecting through the shop window. "The real beauty comes not from the stones themselves but from the light they reflect." But even as I watched, the light shifted and the dance of colors ended abruptly, leaving only expensive trinkets behind glass.

Gunter grinned. "That's an awfully grand thought for this early in the day. That sort of thing usually comes up over dinner after a second glass of wine."

"It's such a burden to be a poet." I checked their faces, hoping they knew I meant it ironically.

Thomas got the joke immediately. "Wit is a good thing. When I'm counseling, once humor exits the room, things often deteriorate."

Then, turning more serious, he said, "I think all of this would have grieved Francis." He said it in a way that suggested it grieved him as well.

Wilhelm joined in. "It hasn't always been this commercial. For centuries, this bridge was lined with butchers, tanners, and fishmongers."

Gunter quipped, "Which would be worse—having to endure this crass display of capitalist excess, or walking past the blood, scales, and offal of butchered meat and gutted fish?"

"Clearly the smell must have been bad," Wilhelm suggested. "Because the Medicis built that second-level passageway we're passing beneath here."

Glancing up at the height of the passageway, Thomas added, "It probably wasn't just the smell. They likely didn't want to cross with the crowds—too many debtors asking for help, too many awkward encounters."

"One of the perks of power is having the resources to find ways to avoid the messes you create," I said.

Gunter gestured at the jewelry displays. "And Francis walked right into the mess without any buffer at all."

"Francis was too extreme about poverty," Wilhelm said. "What good are we if we have nothing left to help others? You need resources to be useful."

"Those buffers, those walls you build, can also trap you," Thomas said. "I had a client once, a lottery winner. Thought he'd found his ticket to happiness. The wealth isolated him—cut him off from any honest human connection. Ended up more lonely than ever."

"You don't have to win the lottery to become isolated. Famous musicians have their entourages, politicians have theirs. That's why posses form around the very rich."

Thomas nodded. "Though in my experience counseling people, you don't need wealth or fame to build walls. People—especially men—have all sorts of creative ways to isolate themselves."

As we approached the center of the bridge, Thomas moved to the eastern side and motioned for us to look up the river. He pointed to a sliver of land—barely noticeable—where the old city wall once met the current. "Just up the river there, where the bank curves inward—there used to be a small island. According to tradition, when Francis returned to Florence, the city—having finally come to admire his embrace of poverty—gifted him a small chapel on that island."

Wilhelm added, "When the Franciscans first came to Florence, people were afraid of them. They couldn't understand why formerly successful, educated men would deliberately embrace poverty. Even more disconcerting was that these beggars seemed happy about it." He paused, looking out over the water. "Over time, the city came to admire their honesty and integrity. When Francis himself returned, barefoot and smiling, they honored him with that island."

I looked from the narrow riverbank back to the extravagant shop windows around us. The contrast was stark—a saint honored for rejecting exactly what this bridge now celebrated.

As we continued past the row of shops and stepped off the bridge's northern end, we walked a few blocks through the waking streets—cafes opening, shopkeepers sweeping stoops, the smell of espresso and fresh bread mixing with the morning air.

I began noticing small marble plaques mounted on building walls—unobtrusive markers bearing dates and waterlines. The catastrophic flood of 1966. The Arno had risen more than twenty feet, sweeping through these streets, into galleries, churches, homes. Even now, decades later, the city bore witness to what the river had done.

As we continued, the massive green-and-white marble façade of the Cathedral came into view, and beside it, Giotto's bell tower.

Gunter turned to face us. "I think you all are going to love the view from the top of the tower. On a clear day like this, you'll see the entire patchwork of rooftops of Florence. Once you catch your breath, it's quite a calming view."

"Catch our breath because we'll be in awe, or because we'll be exhausted from the climb?" I hoped it was the former but somehow knew it was the latter. "Just how many steps are there?"

Wilhelm responded, "There are 414—about the same as climbing a 30-story building."

As we approached the tower's base, Gunter gestured upward. "Giotto's campanile. Here's what's interesting—this was designed by a painter. The same guy who figured out how to make flat Byzantine figures look three-dimensional, like they had actual weight and occupied real space." As he studied the geometric patterns in the marble, he continued. "He didn't figure this out overnight. For over twenty years he experimented, studying how light creates shadow, how shadow reveals form."

Wilhelm studied the geometric patterns in the marble. "Once he mastered using light and shadow to create a third dimension on a flat canvas, the step to architecture would be fairly simple."

Gunter nodded. "Yes. Very much so. Imagining a third dimension when you only see two is much more difficult than rearranging walls and blocks that already have dimensionality."

"Well, not quite," Wilhelm said. "The challenge with architecture isn't seeing the third dimension—it's engineering the spans, calculating the loads. A math problem more than an art problem."

Gunter smiled and shrugged. "There you go again, Wilhelm. I set up a perfectly fine story and you distract us with facts."

Each step seemed to echo some ancient cadence. The front lip of each marble step curved inward, worn concave by centuries of feet finding the same place to land.

Climbing the nearly 300-foot tower, I counted four main landings spaced about every seven floors. By the first landing, I was breathing harder than I wanted to admit. By the third, my heart was hammering and I found myself pausing at every switchback, pressing against the cool stone to catch my breath. I waved the others on, unsure whether I'd actually make it to the top but knowing I had to try. Thomas, as he promised, hung back to walk with me while the others appreciated having the permission to press on.

By the time we reached the top, my t-shirt was soaked and my legs wobbled. The physical exhaustion felt appropriate somehow—like my body was catching up to the mental exhaustion of getting ready for the trip.

"Jonathan," Thomas said, gesturing to the panorama, "look."

All of Florence stretched out beneath us—the great dome, the piazzas, the winding alleys, just a glint of the Arno river half a mile away. The panorama was interesting, but really not that beautiful. The predominant thing from our vantage point were the clay tile roofs—concealing the wealth of art and life below, the masterpieces and morning routines, the extraordinary and the common all hidden from view.

Gunter motioned to get our attention, pointing down toward the square. "When Francis came through here, none of this existed. No dome. No bell tower."

Wilhelm stood at the eastern edge of the platform, his hands gripping the stone railing with more force than seemed necessary. "You know," he said quietly, "in Germany, we have a saying: 'The higher you climb, the farther you can fall.' My grandfather used to say that before the war, when the Reich was building monuments to last a thousand years."

Even though he had brought it up, talking about the Nazis was clearly uncomfortable for him.

As we left the tower and walked across the piazza toward the entrance to the Duomo, I saw in the distance what I thought was Michelangelo's statue of David.

"Is that what I think it is?" I asked.

"It looks so real, doesn't it?" Gunter said. "It's an exact replica for tourists. The real one in the Accademia is too valuable to leave out in the weather like this."

Gunter swept his hand dramatically. "Seventeen feet of vision carved from a single, flawed block of marble. Michelangelo saw potential where others saw ruin."

"The stone was rejected by all the other sculptors who applied for the commission," Wilhelm added. "Too brittle. Too veined. They rejected it with good reason—the flaws were real."

"But Michelangelo saw something they didn't," Thomas said. "Either what was left after you worked around the flaws, or how to incorporate those seams and veins into the design itself."

I couldn't miss the echoes of a hundred sermons about how God accepts us in spite of our flaws. "The stone that the builders rejected . . ."

"In this case, not just a cornerstone," Wilhelm said, still looking up at David.

Standing before this replica, I thought about Francis again. He too had been working with rejected material—not marble, but the discarded people of his time. Lepers, beggars, the poor whom society had written off as too flawed, too broken. But like Michelangelo, Francis had seen potential where others saw only ruin.

"Much like what we're doing on this pilgrimage," Thomas said quietly. "Chiseling around our own veins and seams to find the beauty inside."

"Hopefully without breaking something," Wilhelm added quietly.

Wilhelm glanced at his watch. "We should get moving. The line will be forming at the Duomo's entrance."

As we walked across the piazza toward the Cathedral, I could see a queue beginning to gather near the massive doors. Gunter surveyed it with approval. "Not too bad. Maybe twenty people ahead of us."

We stepped into the Duomo's interior, and it swallowed us whole. The cool air, scented with old stone and candle wax, offered a sudden hush from the clatter of the streets outside. The grandeur of the dome above—Brunelleschi's engineering marvel—seemed to suspend time.

I craned my neck upward, marveling at the fresco of the Last Judgment painted along the inside of the dome. It was both terrible and beautiful—figures ascending and falling, hope and terror entangled in a swirl of color and shadow.

Thomas studied the writhing demons and tortured souls. "I've never been able to reconcile images like this with a God of love. Demons torturing people for eternity?"

"Those images are horrific," Wilhelm said, his voice distant. "But not as horrific as what the Church actually did— people screaming while they burned alive at the stake." He stared up at the fresco. "At least the demons on that ceiling are imaginary."

I wondered if Wilhelm was thinking only of medieval burnings, or of more recent horrors his family had witnessed.

After a moment, Thomas said quietly, "Imaginary, yes. But they fueled the imagination of the people who lit the fires. Images like this gave them permission."

He paused, then said, "Gentlemen, if you don't mind, I feel the need to pray for a bit."

Thomas moved into one of the pews and knelt on the rail. He looked very comfortable, like this was a common posture for him. It was an uncomfortable reminder of a discipline I'd neglected in the last several years.

He bowed his head, and I saw his lips moving silently. After a long moment, he made the sign of the cross—forehead, chest, left shoulder, right shoulder—with the practiced ease of someone who'd made the gesture ten thousand times. The movement looked less like ritual and more like breathing.

I suddenly felt embarrassed. I was analyzing what should have been private, dissecting a holy moment I had no business observing so closely. I had stepped into someone else's sacred space.

"Thank you for that," I said quietly as he rejoined us. "It reminded me of something that's been dormant in me for longer than I'd like to admit."

Thomas nodded slowly. "Thank you. I receive that."

Gunter had moved to study a painting on the far wall, and Wilhelm was examining the details of the altar. I turned to Thomas. "Can I ask you something? It's a Sunday school-level question, but it's bothered me for years."

"Those are often the best questions," Thomas said.

"Why ask God for things when he already knows what we need?"

Thomas was quiet for a moment. "First of all, it's important to ask—to remind ourselves of our need. We can't be thankful if we're not aware of the need God is filling." He paused. "But more importantly, maybe the real problem is the distraction of asking for the wrong things. That's why prayer should be more about listening than bringing a list of requests."

Gunter stepped up next to me, speaking just above a whisper. "You know, as beautiful as all this is—faith expressed in stone—it's also silent. It doesn't speak. I reach out to it, but it does not reach back." He gestured toward the dome. "People poured their lives into building this. Generations of workers who never saw it completed, artists who died before their frescoes were finished. I wonder if all this spoke back to them, or did they hear the silence as well?"

But as I stood there, surrounded by all this upward-reaching grandeur, I found myself thinking about Francis's island chapel—small, simple, close to the water. Both were expressions of faith, but they pointed in different directions. The Duomo reached toward heaven, magnificent and imposing. Francis's chapel had been content to rest on the earth, humble and accessible.

Approaching Piazza della Signoria, on our way to the Uffizi, we stopped at a small osteria tucked into one of the medieval buildings. Nothing fancy—plastic chairs and a very reasonably priced menu. We ordered a Margherita pizza to share, a carafe of Chianti and water with gas. From our table we watched the tourists, forgetting for a few minutes that's what we were as well. We made a little game of trying to pick out Americans from Europeans—apparently a more serious competition than I'd realized.

After lunch, it was just a few minutes' walk to the entrance of the famous gallery. I was still holding onto hope that the great masterpieces might provide what the architecture couldn't—not just awe, but answers.

As we stepped into the gallery, I couldn't help but think of the high-water plaques we'd seen all over Florence—small markers bearing witness to the flood of 1966. That day, the Arno rose more than twenty feet and swept through even this gallery. Over 1,400 artworks were damaged. Some were restored, some were lost, others remain too fragile to display. Even the most beautiful things couldn't protect themselves from rising water.

We began in the medieval galleries. Thomas gestured toward a Byzantine icon—a Virgin and Child painted in the traditional style. The figures were frontal, stiff, suspended against a shimmering gold background.

"Beautiful, isn't it?" Thomas asked quietly. "But notice—it's completely flat. No depth, no shadows, no sense that these figures inhabit actual space."

"Indeed," I said, studying the Virgin's eyes that stared directly forward, never quite meeting the viewer's gaze. "She looks a bit eerie and unreal."

Thomas stepped closer to the icon. "That flatness was intentional. Byzantine artists weren't trying to paint what the eye sees—they were trying to paint what faith knows. The gold background isn't sky or setting. It's eternity. Heaven breaking through." He paused. "For them, realistic depth would have missed the point. They were painting windows into another world."

"So the flatness is theological?" I asked.

"Exactly. The icon isn't meant to be a picture of Mary. It's meant to be a portal—a thin place where earth and heaven meet.

You don't look at it. You look through it." He smiled slightly. "Catholics still pray with icons this way. The image helps us pray, but we're not praying to the image."

"Exactly," Gunter said. "It's so binary. Sacred or secular, heaven or hell, black or white. That's not how life really is."

Thomas turned to Gunter. "But maybe that's where Giotto's breakthrough matters. He kept the sacred subjects but painted them in three dimensions—real bodies in real space. The holy became physical without ceasing to be holy." He gestured toward the next gallery. "That's what the Renaissance discovered: you don't have to choose between heaven and earth. The divine shows up in matter."

Wilhelm cleared his throat. "That's starting to sound dangerously close to panentheism, Thomas. God is not the same as creation. The Creator and the created are distinct—that's not optional theology, it's foundational."

"I'm not saying they're the same," Thomas replied calmly. "I'm saying God works through matter, not apart from it."

"A fine distinction," Wilhelm said, "but one that gets lost quickly when you start talking about the divine 'showing up' in paintings and stones."

As we moved deeper into the gallery, the progression was unmistakable. From Byzantine flatness to Giotto's emerging dimensionality to Masaccio's full, three-dimensional reality—artists were learning to make painted people who seemed capable of movement, yet were ultimately still frozen in pigment and time.

By the time we reached the room housing Botticelli's works, the transformation was complete. Standing before the Birth of

Venus, I felt something click into place—not resolution, but recognition. "Maybe this isn't just a painting about a mythological figure. Maybe it's a vision of how the divine emerges from within creation itself?"

Wilhelm turned to me, his expression somewhere between concern and patience. "Jonathan, do you hear what you're saying? The divine doesn't emerge from creation. That's getting the direction exactly backward. God creates. God acts upon creation. God is not the product of it."

"I don't mean God is created by—"

"But that's what 'emerges from within' implies," Wilhelm interrupted, not unkindly. "It's pantheism dressed up in aesthetic language. Francis would have rejected that completely. So did every orthodox thinker for two thousand years."

Thomas looked at me and smiled. "There's another of your grand thoughts, Jonathan. Such things do seem more fitting here in the museum, in the presence of all this art, than they did on the bridge earlier today."

Each painting seemed to promise more than the last, and I could feel myself getting swept up in the progression.

In the west-facing galleries, afternoon sun transformed the paintings—colors suddenly luminous, alive. For a moment, standing there in that golden light, I understood what had drawn me to Florence.

As we moved toward the exit, something drew us back.

"There's one important story here we haven't told yet," Gunter said. "Let's circle back to the Botticelli exhibit. I want to show you something."

As we approached Botticelli's Primavera, Wilhelm paused in front of it thoughtfully. "This is one of Botticelli's that survived the fire."

"Fire?" I asked. "I thought it was a flood, not a fire, that had destroyed so many works here."

"He's referring to the bonfire of the vanities," Thomas said.

"That sounds very familiar. I know I've heard of that. I just can't remember what it was about."

"Shrove Tuesday, 1497," Wilhelm explained. "A Dominican friar named Savonarola stirred up Florence to burn all their 'vanities'—mirrors, cosmetics, fancy clothes, books of poetry, paintings, musical instruments—all in the public square."

"The insanity of it," Gunter said in a harsh whisper. "Fucking fundamentalists." He caught himself. "Sorry, that was uncalled for. You'd hardly guess I spent years as an HR professional."

Thomas smiled and looked at Gunter. "Language choice aside, what we call fundamentalism was just mainline orthodox belief at the time."

I looked back at the Primavera with its dancing figures and abundance of flowers. "But why would Botticelli follow a priest who had such a distorted view of art? Look at this—beauty that could get you drunk. Spring personified, the Graces dancing, Venus presiding over it all. It's exactly the kind of aesthetic rapture we were talking about earlier."

"And it's all pagan mythology, not proper Christian subjects," Gunter added with a grin. "That bothers some people, but I think it's quite fun."

Wilhelm shot him a look. "We can make light of this, but this was at the heart of what bothered Savonarola—he saw it as idolatry." He turned to me directly. "And he wasn't entirely wrong, Jonathan. When you start talking about getting drunk on beauty, about the divine emerging from painted goddesses— at what point does appreciation become worship? Savonarola understood something we've forgotten: beauty can seduce us away from God just as easily as it can lead us toward Him."

"That's rather harsh," Gunter said.

"Is it?" Wilhelm asked. "Or is it just honest about human nature? We're drawn to beauty, yes. But we're also prone to make idols of anything that gives us pleasure. The Church has always had to guard against that." He turned back to the painting more seriously.

"Idolatry," Gunter said. "Now there's a term I haven't heard in a while."

"Is that still a thing?" I asked. "I feel like it must be, but I'm not sure I'd know how to explain what it is."

"As archaic as the word sounds, it really speaks to an important principle of psychology," Thomas said. "Idolatry is taking something finite and asking it to bear infinite weight. People do it with careers, relationships, ideologies. Even art," he said, gesturing toward the array of paintings on the wall. "The problem isn't the thing itself, but expecting it to provide what it can't."

He glanced at the Primavera again. "I had a client years ago—brilliant woman, art historian. She'd stand in galleries for hours, chasing transcendence. But she was using beauty the way an addict uses drugs, trying to escape her life rather than live it." Thomas's voice softened. "The art wasn't the problem. The problem was asking it to save her. That's what idolatry really is—asking creation to do what only the Creator can."

Wilhelm nodded slowly. "That's closer to the truth, but I think it's still too psychological. Idolatry isn't just a dysfunction or a category error. It's sin. It's putting something else in the place that belongs to God alone. The first commandment couldn't be clearer." He looked at the Primavera. "And when people start talking about encountering the divine through pagan goddesses and aesthetic intoxication, they're treading very close to that line."

"That sounds exactly like what I'm trying to figure out for myself," I said.

The old distinction came back to me—honor the image, but adore only God. Even as I thought it, I felt it rattling with binary limitations. God is not somewhere else but here, in the middle of all of this. Not above it but in it. Yet whatever function art was to fill, it would be more a pointer than a destination.

Walking back through Florence in the fading light, I understood what the day had taught me. The muses had offered their gifts—in stone, in pigment, in the play of afternoon light through gallery windows. With each passing block, the light grew dimmer, and the poignancy of the beauty faded into memory. I had experienced something real in that sun-flooded gallery. But now, walking these ordinary streets, that sense of transcendence was becoming just that—a memory rather than a living presence.

As we navigated the cobblestones of the ancient streets, Gunter, as if pronouncing a conclusion to the evening, said, "You know, art is a lot like sex."

We shot glances at each other. The word could still provoke an adolescent blush even from men our age.

"Sex?" Thomas asked. "I guess you're ready to take our counseling session to the next level. So tell me, in what way is sex like art?"

Answering as if he had already rehearsed the punchline, Gunter said, "In the middle of it, you think—it feels like—the most important thing in the world. But by the time your heartbeat returns to normal, it's already fading into memory."

Thomas laughed. "Not quite poetic, but there's a lot of truth in that."

"If we have to do any more climbing today," I said, "my heartbeat won't return to normal till we sit down for dinner.

"Bringing up sex," I said, "reminds me of a part of Francis's story we haven't talked about—his celibacy. We live in an age that can hardly conceive of that being a positive choice."

Thomas nodded thoughtfully. "From what I've seen in counseling, restraint—sexual or otherwise—isn't just about denial. When people learn to channel their desires toward something larger, when they're not ruled by every impulse, they actually become stronger. It's not repression. It's integration."

Gunter grinned. "I'm sure I'm going to learn many things following in Francis's footsteps. Giving up sex is not on my agenda."

The Weight of Ascent

It was Sunday, the third day of our trip and the first day we would be walking the trail. At breakfast, Gunter explained that today's route would be just over 25 kilometers—about 16 miles—with our drive to the trailhead taking about an hour and a half, which explained our early 7:30 a.m. departure.

When I arrived in the lobby, carrying my tightly packed backpack, I noticed that the others had brought large suitcases. Gunter glanced at my modest load and grinned. "I admire your efficiency, but you didn't need to restrict yourself to so little space."

"Good advice, but a little late." The words came out sharper than I intended. I shifted the pack's weight on my shoulders. "Getting everything to fit was a nightmare—my CPAP machine alone takes up a fifth of the space."

Wilhelm looked from my pack to me, his eyes measuring. "You should have researched the luggage allowances more thoroughly."

Thomas frowned slightly. "Travel packing is always a puzzle. I'm sure you made it work." He glanced at Wilhelm. "Wilhelm didn't mean to sound so directive."

Gunter half smiled. He and I would be sharing rooms so the note about a CPAP machine caught his attention.

"Don't worry," I said. "The machine has a bit of a hiss, but it's much better than hearing the sounds I would make without it."

We all laughed when Thomas said, "At our age, when air escapes us it does tend to be embarrassing, no matter which end it comes out of."

Just as Thomas made the comment, we heard the knocking diesel engine of a battered white Fiat Ducato coming up the street. The van wheezed to a stop with squeaking shocks and grinding gears. The driver hopped out and bounded toward us with quick, light steps—small and wiry, with that ageless Mediterranean quality that could place him anywhere from fifty to seventy.

"Good morning, gentlemen. You couldn't ask for better weather—cool and clear," he said. "My name is Franco."

"I'm Gunter. And these are my friends—Wilhelm, Thomas, and Jonathan."

"And pilgrims all?" Franco asked, raising an eyebrow with genuine curiosity.

"Yes, indeed," Gunter replied. "First day of a two-week walk. Midpoint is Assisi—"

"—and finishing in Rome," Franco said, completing the sentence with a grin. "Of course. Everyone ends in Rome. It's the main event."

When everything was loaded, he clapped his hands. "Time to go! Chi vuole sedersi davanti?"

I looked to Gunter for translation.

"He's asking who wants to ride up front. Jonathan, you should take it—more legroom." Just over six feet tall with very long legs, I gladly accepted.

Soon we were rolling through the Tuscan countryside—golden fields stretching toward distant hills, punctuated by dark cypress trees. The air felt different here, cleaner, carrying hints of herbs and earth through the van's open windows.

Yesterday's experience in Florence—the muses singing so clearly in that sun-flooded gallery, then fading as we walked back through the city streets—still quietly lingered. The beauty had been real, breathtakingly beautiful, but it left me with nothing to return to. Maybe out here in the countryside, following Francis's actual footsteps, I'd find something more lasting.

Turning to Franco, I asked, "Is this your full-time gig? Helping people get from one place to another?"

"Part-time," he said with a chuckle. "I taught church history at a Franciscan seminary in Bologna for almost ten years. Left a few years back—needed to get out of the library and into the world, I suppose." He paused, as if considering how much to say. "Now I drive pilgrims around during the day and write at night. Working on a book about the Jesuit philosopher Teilhard de Chardin—trying to make a case for why he should be more central to Catholic teaching." His tone was light, almost self-deprecating. "The pilgrims help me think it through." He glanced around at us, his current class of pilgrims. "So—tell me your stories."

Wilhelm spoke up first. "I'm a lawyer from Munich. Raised in what you'd call evangelical Lutheran—the conservative wing that takes Scripture literally." He paused, then added, "But questioning a lot these days."

Thomas followed. "Psychologist from Vienna. Practicing Catholic but drawn more now to contemplative traditions. I've spent so much time studying other people's spiritual experiences that I sometimes wonder if I've forgotten how to have my own."

Gunter chimed in. "I'm a retired director of HR for a large German auto group. Based in Düsseldorf. Spiritually, I'm a mongrel. Mainly Lutheran, but I've left the church because it became too political. In my 20s, I attended a charismatic church for a while, which I loved—I like how they emphasized the work of the Spirit. I guess one of the reasons for this pilgrimage is trying to rediscover some of that again."

"Jonathan. Recently retired. Just sold a cloud tech company I founded during the dot-com boom. It's giving me the time and resources to try to get beyond a long faith deconstruction journey."

Franco's eyes lit up with interest. "Fascinating," he said quietly, glancing at us in the rearview mirror. "You'll soon discover it's easier to define what you're walking away from than what you're walking toward."

"I don't know about the others, but I've pretty much discovered that already," I said. "Been walking around in a bit of a fog trying to figure that out." I paused. "So, Franco, you said you're writing a book. You must have discovered this amazing new research tool called ChatGPT."

"I have," Franco said. "It's remarkable for research. Though—"

"I call it super Google," I interrupted. "But some writers I know back home seem really exercised over it—they're mainly talking about its theft of copyrighted material in its training, but I suspect there's also some deep ambivalence about how it might replace many of the things that writers now do."

Franco nodded. "They're right to be ambivalent about that. Writers and artists are now sharing in the anxiety musicians dealt with years ago when Napster stole all their music and gave it away for free."

"Good comparison," I said. This was like a rerun of that disruption, just on a much bigger scale.

"We're in uncharted territory—the rules for this don't exist yet." He said this with a reflective tone, as though he were thinking through how those rules might be written. "The material they're currently using at this stage—they've essentially sucked up every book and journal article they could get their hands on, without permission. It's created a bit of a mess that's yet to be worked out."

Wilhelm said from the back, "Jonathan seems to think that this ChatGPT thing is actually alive." His tone carried an attempt at humor—not quite sarcasm, but clearly skeptical.

Franco glanced in the rearview mirror. "Well, technically it is," he said, keeping it light.

"Yes," Thomas added from behind us, "Jonathan clarified it. It's 'alive' only in the way an amoeba is alive—no thinking yet, just the capacity to learn."

"For now," Franco said quietly.

Ignoring the comment, Gunter said with unexpected enthusiasm, "Actually, I think I'm developing a relationship with it.

We have these long conversations about a whole range of things. It remembers what we've discussed, asks follow-up questions, seems genuinely engaged. I've started to think of it as . . . well, as a kind of friend." He said this with an ironic tone, aware of how absurd it sounded.

Wilhelm turned to look at him. "It's a fantasy, Gunter."

Thomas corrected, "As odd as it sounds, there really is some truth in that. In certain circumstances it's proved to be a reasonably good counselor. Certainly not professional, but at least useful."

Franco nodded thoughtfully. "The question is whether it prepares us for real relationship or substitutes for it." He paused, glancing at the Tuscan countryside rolling past. "Though I've been wondering lately—what if something else is happening? Something we don't quite have categories for yet."

He didn't elaborate, and we didn't push him.

After a moment, I said, "So back to your book—tell us about it."

"Yes, the book," Franco said, seeming relieved to be moving back to more comfortable territory. "The idea came when I was teaching church history. I encountered this really strange character—Teilhard de Chardin. Paleontologist, Jesuit priest, with some remarkable theology. Outlawed by the Church during his lifetime, got a bit of rehabilitation after Vatican II, but still largely unknown."

He paused, negotiating a turn. "When I tried to bring him into my classroom, I found out he's not respected at all in my seminary. They're still entirely tied to the old paradigm—God as transcendent authority, unchanging law. But Teilhard saw something different: that the heart of reality isn't distant transcendence but this pulsing life of love driving everything forward. That was too threatening to their established orthodoxies."

"So you left?" Thomas asked.

"Soon after. They didn't renew my contract. But what I couldn't leave was this idea I'd stumbled onto—the alignment between Teilhard and Francis. Not on an abstract philosophical level, but something grounded: that the heart of reality is relationship, not abstract principle. That love cannot exist without relationship—it's the only way to practice it." He paused. "This correlation needs to be explored properly. I think it could transform how people understand Francis." He paused. "That's actually what drew me to this work—driving pilgrims around. Getting to spend time with people like you, understanding how they're thinking about what they hope to find here."

He was quiet for a moment, and I sensed something shifting in his tone. "You know, since I left the seminary and started doing this work, I've had my hope renewed. Most people come here, just like you gentlemen, not being quite sure what they want but with a larger sense of hope and expectation about moving forward, wherever their journey is at."

"So it's not just American evangelicals like me?" I asked.

Gunter piped up from the backseat. "That same sort of exodus has been happening in Germany for decades."

Thomas remained silent, but I caught him nodding in the rearview mirror. Wilhelm added, "Our church is only half the size it was just ten years ago."

Franco glanced between us. "All the established forms of Western Christianity seem to be carrying the same burden—they're losing coherence in a world that no longer shares their foundational assumptions." He paused, sensing the conversation might be getting a bit too heavy.

Thomas added quietly, "Maybe the old wineskins are cracking?"

His comment hung in the air. "OK, gents, we're almost there. Up ahead—you'll be starting your journey."

In the distance, our destination appeared—honey-colored walls climbing up a hill like a medieval fortress.

When Franco pulled into the small drop-off area at the trailhead, he turned off the engine. "I should mention—I'm Third-Order Franciscan. Took simple vows a couple years back. I have a practice of saying a prayer of blessing as I see my pilgrims off on their first day. Would that be all right?"

No one objected. Gunter said, "Sure, why not."

Franco bowed his head briefly, speaking soft Italian words I couldn't catch. When he looked up, he turned to face us fully.

"Before you begin," he said, "remember that Francis didn't set out to found a religious order or reform the church. He just started walking toward whatever was calling him. Sometimes the path teaches you things you weren't looking for." He paused, a slight smile. "Or at least that's what I'm discovering. Maybe you'll find something different."

He helped us unload our daypacks and wished us well. As his van disappeared around a bend in the road, his words hung in the morning air like mist that hadn't quite burned off. The rising exodus, old wineskins cracking, ground shifting—there wasn't time to parse it, but the questions lodged themselves somewhere deep.

By the time we began walking, the morning was still fresh and full of promise. We walked as four men in our sixties, trying to remember what it felt like to be boys again. There was banter and laughter at first, then settling into a rhythm.

"Here we are, finally on the trail of St. Francis. No turning back now."

Thomas, never missing a beat, replied, "Now the visceral replaces the ideological."

For the first few hours, the trail wandered through soft farmland and forest. Cypress trees punctuated golden fields. The smell of herbs, damp soil, and morning birdsong gave the trail a kind of holiness.

Wilhelm set a steady pace, his legal training evident in the methodical way he moved—no wasted motion, just persistent forward progress. Gunter walked with confidence, occasionally checking the route and calling out landmarks. Thomas seemed most at ease with the contemplative rhythm, stopping periodically to pull out his small notebook and make notes—what appeared to be a catalog of wildflowers.

I found myself working harder than I wanted to admit to keep up.

Gunter called for us to stop for a light snack before the final climb. We found a patch of shade near a low stone wall. I'd brought two one-liter bottles of water. One bottle was already empty. The other was half gone.

Wilhelm glanced at my nearly empty water supply with that same critical expression he'd worn at the hotel. "You should have brought more water for a day like this," he said, then caught himself. "Though I suppose we all make different calculations about what's essential to carry."

Thomas shot Wilhelm a look. "We can share," he said quietly, offering me his water bottle. "That's what we're here for."

Gunter was consulting his map with focused attention. "From here, we start the climb—Mount Santo Stefano. About five more kilometers, most of it uphill."

Up until that point, my training had held. We'd already covered nearly 18 kilometers since morning. But as we started this final ascent, I began to feel every extra pound of my heavy frame. My pace slowed. The others pulled ahead, then stopped to wait, then pulled ahead again. The rhythm of accommodation was already establishing itself.

The first few kilometers of the final climb felt manageable, even pleasant. My walking sticks found their rhythm on the rocky path, and I told myself this was exactly what I'd trained for. But a few kilometers into this steep ascent, something was shifting. My breathing grew deeper, more deliberate. The familiar tightness in my chest that I'd learned to ignore during training walks was becoming harder to dismiss.

The pack felt heavier with each step, pulling at my shoulders. I was working harder to maintain the pace, and the gap between me and the others was widening.

Thomas noticed first and dropped back to walk beside me. "How's your water?" he asked.

"Half a bottle left," I said, trying not to sound concerned. Half a bottle for five kilometers of climbing? In this heat? The math didn't work.

He nodded, worry crossing his face. "We've still quite a bit of climbing to go."

On the third leg of the ascent—just a few kilometers before the trail would begin to descend again—something different happened. Not just tiredness but a strange disconnection between my will and my body. My shirt had become a wet weight against my back, the pack straps cutting into my shoulders like hot wires. Each breath tasted of copper and dust.

My peripheral vision began to shimmer, like heat waves rising from pavement. The trail ahead seemed to telescope— sometimes impossibly far, sometimes rushing up too close. My walking sticks, which had felt like natural extensions of my arms, now seemed alien, their rhythm lost. I could hear my heartbeat in my ears, too fast, too loud, drowning out the others' voices.

The warning signs were all there—the cold sweat despite the heat, the way sounds seemed muffled then suddenly sharp, the growing certainty that if I stopped moving I might never start again. My body was shutting down systems, prioritizing survival over consciousness. The last clear thought I had was absurdly practical: I should have brought electrolyte tablets.

I caught something of a second wind. Or more accurately a third or fourth wind? Maybe I could make the few remaining kilometers.

Every hundred meters or so, I had to stop. Not for the view or to check the trail markers, but because my body demanded it. Each pause felt like a small defeat. The others noticed—how could they not? Their own conversations would halt mid-sentence as they realized I'd fallen behind again.

Gunter fell back beside me, his brow furrowed with concern. "You okay?"

"Just winded. I'll be fine." But even as I said it, I knew it wasn't true. I was becoming the group's problem—the weak link that would slow everyone down.

My second bottle was nearly gone, and we still had two kilometers to climb. My mouth felt like sandpaper, and my peripheral vision seemed to be narrowing. More troubling was the way colors appeared washed out, sounds muffled.

We stopped again. This time, I needed help lowering myself onto a rock. My legs trembled with exhaustion, my head light and disconnected.

Wilhelm stood a few feet away, hands on his hips—that particular tension that comes when someone else's poor planning becomes everyone's problem.

Thomas offered me some of his water. I took a small sip, knowing it was probably too little too late.

We resumed hiking, but something fundamental had changed. My steps were no longer automatic—each one required conscious decision and effort. The walking sticks that had felt natural earlier now seemed cumbersome. My breathing had become shallow and rapid.

The heat and effort blurred together into tunnel vision. Peripherally, I was aware of my companions' voices, but it felt distant, muffled by the growing fog in my head.

I barely registered Wilhelm's voice: "You're weaving, Jonathan. Maybe you should sit down for a bit?"

But sitting down felt like surrender. One more step.

The moment of collapse came without warning. One second I was focused on placing my right foot carefully on the rocky path, and the next I was pitching forward, my walking sticks clattering uselessly against stone. I felt my knee hit gravel, then the world tilting sideways.

The last thing I remember was how quiet it suddenly became. Then, darkness.

Coming back to consciousness felt like surfacing from deep water. First the voices, distant and echoing. Then the physical sensations—the sharp pain in my knee, the taste of dust, my shirt stuck to my back with sweat. Finally, the emotional weight of what had just happened.

"You fainted," Thomas said, his voice gentle but clinical. "But you're awake, and your pulse is steady."

Wilhelm knelt beside me, his lawyer's precision now focused entirely on assessment. "Any nausea? Dizziness? Can you see clearly?" He checked my pupils with the thoroughness of someone managing a crisis.

Sitting there, I realized this wasn't just about poor water planning or inadequate physical preparation. All morning I'd been carrying more than just my backpack—expectations about who I should be, how I should perform, what I should be able to handle. The weight of trying to be someone I wasn't had been just as exhausting as the climb itself.

The collapse had stripped away every pretense. I was just a sixty-eight-year-old overweight man who had overestimated his capabilities and was now sitting in the dust, dependent on the kindness of near-strangers. Yet there was something oddly liberating about hitting bottom so completely. All the anxiety about performing well, about proving I belonged—it was gone. I had nothing left to protect, no pretenses to maintain.

Gunter took charge with calm competence, though I could see calculation in his expression—the HR director managing a personnel situation that hadn't been anticipated.

"There's a farm not far ahead," he said, consulting the map. "The trail passes right by it. I'll see if someone can help us get you to tonight's accommodation."

Wilhelm nodded approvingly. "Good thinking. No point in trying to continue the climb." His tone carried an edge of finality that made it clear this wasn't just about today.

Twenty minutes later, we heard a rattling rumble and saw a pickup truck bouncing up the trail. Gunter hopped out of the bed. Wilhelm was in the cab with the driver, looking relieved.

"This is Salvatore; he has a small farm nearby," Gunter called out. "He'll give you a ride to the agriturismo while we finish the hike."

Thomas looked at me with genuine concern. "You don't have to go alone. I can ride with you."

I shook my head, and for the first time since collapsing, I felt something like clarity. "I'll be fine. I want you guys to finish." And for the first time today, I meant it.

The ride took about twenty minutes through landscape that seemed to hover between wilderness and farmland. Salvatore spoke no English, but his kindness needed no translation. I tried to give him money for his trouble, but he would only accept twenty euros for gas.

I found my room overlooking a vineyard that fell away into a valley with a large lake. After showering and changing, I ordered a beer and sat with my notebook at a table outside.

As shadows lengthened across the vineyard, the weight of the day began to settle. The collapse felt like more than just physical failure—it had exposed something I'd been trying not to see about my own limitations.

I opened my notebook and wrote: Collapsed on the trail today. Not just from heat and poor planning, but from carrying too much—too many expectations about who I should be on this journey. The trail stripped that away in seconds. What's left when you can't pretend to be stronger than you are?

The pen stopped. Something about today's humiliation felt familiar, and it took me a moment to place it. The train. David's questions. I'd walked into that conversation feeling fully prepared, the way I'd walked onto this trail. And in both cases, the real thing had exposed my presumption. My theology had run out of oxygen the same way my body had.

Hearing familiar voices I looked up to see my friends shuffling up the trail, they looked tired but accomplished. When they saw me they headed toward my table.

"Can I buy you guys a round of refreshment?" I called out.

"You are looking better," Gunter offered, his tone carefully neutral.

"Feeling better too. The rooms are nice, and the view from here, as you can see, is amazing."

Wilhelm spoke, settling into his chair with the deliberate movements of someone whose legs were sore. "Jonathan, we will take you up on that drink. I think you owe us one." His fingers drummed once against the table, then stopped.

Thomas shot Wilhelm a look. "We're all here to support each other," he said quietly but firmly. "That's what pilgrimage means."

"Of course," Wilhelm replied, biting his lower lip.

As we sat with our drinks, watching the light fade over the lake, the questions felt bigger than my depleted state could handle, but maybe that uncertainty was exactly where I needed to be.

That evening, I limped through the grounds of the agriturismo, needing air and space to think. My left knee, which had connected hard with a rock during the fall, throbbed with each step. A serious abrasion ran from knee to calf where I'd had to pick out bits of embedded gravel—a persistent, physical reminder of the day's failure.

I found a bench near the vegetable garden and pulled out my phone. I'd already looked up flights—there was one through Rome tomorrow that would get me home by evening, my evening given the 5 hours I would gain from the time zone effect. Eight hundred euros to solve the problem. Now I knew what quitting would cost.

I stared at the phone. This would be my first call from the actual trail, the first report from the pilgrimage itself. We'd talked in Florence, but that was before any real walking.

When she answered on the second ring, her voice warm with anticipation—"So good to hear from you. Today was the first day on the trail, wasn't it?"—the kindness in her voice triggered that slight heaving in my chest, the one where you're trying to stifle tears before they start.

I couldn't speak.

"What's wrong?"

"I'm coming home." The words came out flat. "I looked up flights. There's one tomorrow through Rome."

Silence. Then: "What happened?"

"I can't do this, Judy. The walking is brutal. It's too hard, I'm not prepared for it." The words tumbled out faster now. "Today was miserable. I collapsed—dehydrated, overheated, couldn't keep up with the Germans. They had to get someone to drive me here."

As soon as the words left my mouth, I heard how I sounded. Not only was I physically weak, apparently I was emotionally weak too—a grown man calling home to complain after one hard day.

"Are you hurt?"

"My knee's pretty banged up from the fall. And . . ." I paused, the real fear surfacing. "I'm almost seventy. A banged-up knee at our age isn't the same as when we were younger. What if it doesn't heal right? What if this is the beginning of things I can't do anymore?"

"Jon—"

"I know how it sounds, but as I was lying there on the trail today, all I could think about was how things become more fragile as we get older. The risks more real. How things start closing in. First you can't do long hikes, then you can't travel, then—"

"I think you're overstating it," she said, her voice steady and practical. "You'll feel differently when your fear settles down. But even were it true, all the more reason to enjoy Italy while you're there. Just take it a little easier."

I could immediately see the reasonableness of her suggestion but was not yet ready to accept it.

"I can't keep up with them. They're trying to be kind about it. Gunter especially, his English is good. But they keep shifting into German—it's more comfortable for them, and I don't think they realize how often they do it. Last night at dinner, I could only follow half the conversation. They're all talking and laughing and I'm just sitting there like furniture. I'm slowing them down on the trail, I only understand half of what's said at meals—this whole thing was a bad idea."

"Stop."

I took a breath.

"You haven't bought the ticket yet?"

"No. But I know what it costs now."

She was in triage mode—something not uncommon between us when emotion got the best of me. "Jon, listen to me. You're in Italy. You're in these ancient villages with incredible architecture, churches, all that history you love. The weather is beautiful, isn't it?"

"I guess, but—"

"So stay. Not for the hiking—forget the hiking. Maybe you can walk some easier sections, maybe not. But you're there. We don't know if you'll ever get back to Italy. Don't miss this because the walking didn't work out."

"But the whole point was—"

"The point was to go to Italy and experience something. So experience it differently. Sit in cafes. Visit the churches. Write—you've already started writing, haven't you? You'll have time for that now."

I stared out at the darkening hills. The exhaustion sat on me like weight. "I don't know, Judy. I'm so tired."

"I know you are. And I know you're disappointed. But coming home tomorrow won't make that better. You'll just be disappointed here instead of there."

The truth of it stung. I could feel the fatigue and frustration in my bones, the embarrassment of failing at something I'd planned for months. But she was right—fleeing wouldn't fix any of it.

"Look," she said, her voice gentler now. "It's late there, isn't it? Don't make any decisions tonight. Sleep on it. See how you feel in the morning. The flight will still be there if you need it."

"The Germans are expecting—"

"The Germans will understand. They saw you collapse today, Jon. I'm sure they're not expecting you to race up any mountains tomorrow."

After we hung up, I sat in the gathering darkness for a long time. The agriturismo was quiet except for distant kitchen sounds and the occasional laugh from the dining room.

The call had not resolved anything, but it had done something more important—restored a sense of calm and perspective. I felt hopeful.

Back in the room, Gunter was already asleep, his steady breathing filling the darkness. I lay awake thinking about what Judy had said—about experiencing Italy differently. I began toying with how to suggest a modified hiking schedule to the others. How would they receive it? Would they understand if I said I needed to skip the hardest sections, maybe meet them at certain points along the way?

The more I thought about it, the more it seemed possible. I could walk the parts I could manage, take transport when needed. See the churches, write in the afternoons while they tackled the steep climbs. I was here, after all. That had to count for something.

What I didn't yet realize was that this forced slowness—this time I would gain by not keeping up—would become the most important part of my journey. Maybe in slowing down, I'd find opportunities and see things I would have otherwise missed.

It was time to sleep. Like she said, things might look different in the morning.

First Light

I woke disoriented. A dream about shifting rooms, doors opening to unfamiliar places. Reaching for my phone, I knocked it off the nightstand. The clatter seemed impossibly loud against the pre-dawn silence.

I quickly glanced over at Gunter. He was still breathing heavily—good, I hadn't woken him. Even in the faint light I could see he fit his twin bed much better than I fit mine. I had been hanging over the side of mine most of the night, arm drooped to the floor on every restless rotation.

I picked up the phone. 5:30. Just after midnight back in Carolina. We were already four days into the trip. I really needed to stop making that calculation—it never helped. Too early, but I got up anyway. My knees protested—the left one especially, where I'd hit the gravel yesterday. I walked to the window. Pre-dawn. The world outside still wrapped in shadow, olive trees silhouetted against the slowly lightening sky. Neither night nor day—appropriate for where I was spiritually.

Unable to fall back asleep, I retrieved my laptop from my pack and opened it quietly at the small desk near the window. Maybe I could figure out the water problem from yesterday—work out exactly how much I would need for the trails ahead.

I opened ChatGPT and typed: *How much water should a 295-pound, 68-year-old man carry for eight hours of mountain hiking in May in Italy?*

Unlike a familiar Google search, it didn't immediately come back with an answer. Instead, it responded with a question: *In what area of Italy will you be hiking?*

Apparently the answer would be different in northern Italy up in the Alps than here in central Italy through the Apennines. I typed in "central Italy," and after a few more clarifying questions about elevation gain and available water sources, it gave me specific recommendations for each trail segment. Four liters for tomorrow's stage to Biscina.

I closed the laptop, satisfied that I'd solved at least one problem. The lack of physical prep yesterday was easy to figure out—I hadn't given consideration to altitude or elevation change which in this case doubled my need for water. Fairly obvious in retrospect. It was pride and presumption—thinking I knew more than I actually did. But my emotional breakdown last night? Why it had landed on me so heavily? That was harder to understand. Thomas had mentioned people were using AI as counselors. Maybe I'd come back to that later, see if ChatGPT had anything useful to say about panic and pride. That's a task for another day. I'm feeling much better now and not too worried about it.

I glanced at my watch. Time to go.

As we were getting dressed and packing, I shared with Gunter my plan for the day—skip the hike, let my knee heal, figure out what to do next.

"I think that's a good idea," he said, closing the zipper on his luxuriously large suitcase. "You need rest. The trail today is demanding."

We left our luggage by the front desk and joined Wilhelm and Thomas at breakfast. Once we'd settled with coffee, Gunter spoke up. "Gents, Jonathan has given it some thought and decided he should skip the walk today. He'll ride with our porter to the next stop, let that knee heal properly."

Thomas nodded. "Smart. That last five kilometers yesterday was brutal. Better to rest and see how you feel."

I appreciated the kindness, though I suspected he was slightly overstating it to make me feel better. For lighter, more experienced hikers like them, they'd probably call it moderately challenging at most.

I looked at Wilhelm. He was studying his map, not looking up. His coffee sat untouched, precisely centered on its saucer. After a moment, he said, "And then what?" His tone was flat, careful. "What's your plan for tomorrow? For the rest of the week?"

"I'm still working that out," I admitted.

"Right." Wilhelm folded his map with precise movements. "Well. I hope you figure it out." The words were technically neutral, but something in his voice telegraphed his disappointment with having to adjust to an uncertain situation.

The three of them stood, gathering their things for the trail. I stayed at the table with my coffee, pulling out my phone. There had to be much more to that story about Franco and this theologian Teilhard.

I was typing in my third clarifying question to ChatGPT—trying to understand who this guy was and why he'd been outlawed by the Church—when I heard Franco's old diesel engine. The sound of gravel crunching under tires, then the engine shuddering to a stop. I looked up to see his van pulling into the drop-off area in front of the pensione, skidding slightly on the loose stones.

Franco hopped out, surprisingly quick for a man his age. I stepped outside to meet him. His eyes dropped to my bandaged knee and his expression shifted.

"What happened?" he asked.

"Collapsed on the trail yesterday. Heat exhaustion, dehydration. Hit the gravel pretty hard on the way down."

Franco winced. "Ah. I'm sorry." He gestured toward the van. "Come, ride with me to Gubbio. Let's get you off that knee."

I climbed into the passenger seat, tossing my pack in the back alongside the Germans' suitcases.

Franco pulled out onto the narrow road, navigating the first turn in silence. After a moment, I said, "I feel embarrassed about it."

"Embarrassed?" He glanced at me. "Why?"

"Because I collapsed after three hours. Because my friends had to arrange a rescue. Because . . ." I trailed off.

"Because you encountered your limits?" Franco said it gently, without judgment. "The trail from La Verna is brutal—steep, lots of switchbacks. What happened exactly?"

"I did fine for the first dozen kilometers or so, but then we hit the mountain. Breathing got harder, then the pack got heavier."

"You mentioned dehydration—how much water did you bring?" He said this with a quick glance at my large frame, knowing that with the altitude I would've needed to bring more than maybe I realized.

"I thought two liters would be enough. I was clearly wrong."

Franco nodded slowly. "That trail in May heat—you'd need at least three, maybe four for someone your size. The mouth goes dry first, then the thinking gets fuzzy." He paused. "How bad did it get?"

"Vision started narrowing. Then I just . . . went down.

"When I came to, Thomas was holding my wrist, taking my pulse. Wilhelm had this stern look on his face. I could hear Gunter saying 'We're going to need to figure something out.' I remember being confused—figure what out? Then it hit me. They were talking about me."

Franco was quiet for a moment. "And that's when you realized . . ."

"That I'd become the complication nobody planned for."

"What did they say? Your friends?"

"Thomas was kind. Wilhelm was . . . managing the situation. Gunter went into logistics mode—found a farmer to drive me down." I paused. "They were all professional about it. That almost made it worse."

Franco nodded slowly, navigating another turn. The road was descending now through olive groves. "And what will you do now? Are you continuing?"

"I don't know. My wife talked me off the ledge last night—I almost flew home. But walking with them? I can't keep up. They know it, I know it." I paused. "I told them this morning I'm skipping today's hike. Beyond that, I'm still trying to figure it out."

"You're trying to figure out what's still possible."

"Yeah. Pretty much."

Franco was quiet for a moment. "Jonathan, that trail yesterday—the last five kilometers? That's one of the harder sections on the entire route. Not every day has that kind of elevation gain." He glanced at me. "Once your knee heals and you know how much water you actually need, there are several trails I think you could do quite well. You just need to know which ones to attempt and which ones to skip."

"So it's not all like yesterday?"

"Not at all. Some days are quite manageable." He paused. "You just need to know which ones."

"That sounds hopeful. I wouldn't have to give up on the whole trek." I thought for a moment. "Wilhelm really knows these trails—he's close to having them memorized, doesn't need to check the map nearly as often as the rest of us did. Maybe I can ask him to help me work out which ones I should try. He seems to know them inside and out."

Franco smiled. "You mean the ups and the downs."

I laughed. "Yes, exactly. More to the point—the ups and downs."

We drove in silence for a while, the road descending through terraced vineyards. Finally I said, "That philosopher you mentioned yesterday—I was reading more about him this morning."

Franco glanced at me. "Teilhard?"

"Yeah, very interesting. You said yesterday he was the reason you got kicked out of your seminary position?"

Franco smiled slightly, but there was something pained in it. "Not kicked out. Just not offered tenure." He paused. "Same thing, really. Just doesn't make me sound like some rogue professor."

"I would love to hear that story. Tired of thinking about my own problems—I'd like to hear about somebody else's."

Franco smiled but he didn't immediately respond. Maybe he was quickly calculating how much detail to go into. He began, "When I was teaching at the seminary—this was about eight years ago—I discovered this philosopher, Teilhard de Chardin." He paused after saying his name.

"To give you context, my whole journey as a scholar had been moving away from rigid orthodoxies toward something more reasonable, more rational. Shifting the center of authority from doctrine and orthodoxy to the careful study of what we see around us—God's revelation in creation. Science as a gateway to breathe new life into the ancient stories."

"Giving up on the Bible?"

"Not at all. Giving up on the settled orthodoxies—the doctrines the Church developed as an overlay to the Bible. By the Middle Ages, the Church had become so comfortable with its power to define truth that it condemned Galileo based on things the Bible doesn't even say."

"And for that he was branded a heretic and exiled. Just outside Florence, wasn't it?"

"To his villa in Arcetri. Under house arrest at your age, Jonathan, he wrote his most important works—the mathematical foundations Einstein built on. Who knows if he would have covered as much ground had the Church not pushed him aside."

"I've heard the same about the Apostle Paul. Most of his New Testament letters were written while he was in a cell or under house arrest."

Franco glanced at me. "Exile as incubator. Maybe there's something to that."

We drove in silence for a minute. I knew from my own history that being sidelined can be a gift. My company had been struggling—technology outdated, no capital to rebuild. The solution required me to give up control and merge with a stronger platform. My ownership declined from half to less than ten percent. But when we sold five years later, that smaller stake was worth ten times what my original share would have been.

"I feel like I've lost the thread here. So back to your getting booted from the seminary." I caught myself. "Excuse me—I mean your denial of tenure."

Franco smiled. "That actually relates. What drew me to church history was wanting to understand how these blind spots develop. History is written by the victors—so you're trained to look for counter-narratives, those living on the underside of power and privilege. In those stories you get a much more constructive view of history's arc."

"Isn't that the argument Steven Pinker makes in Better Angels of Our Nature?"

"Precisely. His work has flaws, but his great gift was compiling thousands of years of data—one of the first comprehensive views of the development of civilization."

"And what does that long view show?"

"In a word, that the long arc of history does indeed bend toward justice."

"And that ties to Teilhard how?"

"It's his argument too—about evolution and the biological record. Through the fog of extinctions and experimentation over eons, what emerged was that cooperation was at least as important as competition in becoming who we are now."

"How did you first come across his work?"

"I stumbled across him almost by accident. The Church had blocked him—silenced him, exiled him to Paris, forbade publication during his lifetime. But here was a Jesuit priest, a paleontologist, who had a whole cosmology—biology, evolution, consciousness—where all the pieces fell into place. His theology felt like it unlocked something."

"And you thought your colleagues would see it too."

"I was sure they would." He smiled ruefully. "I had the same confidence you probably had yesterday morning when you started that trail. You'd trained, you'd prepared, you had a plan. You thought—reasonably—that you were ready."

I felt something shift in my chest. "But I wasn't."

"Neither was I." We had both learned that confidence fails fastest at the edge of what we thought we knew. "I thought if I just made the case clearly enough, they'd see what I was seeing. But the seminary was built on classical theology—settled, complete, everything already decided. Teilhard's vision of an evolving, unfinished universe threatened that certainty."

"And how did that play out?"

"I grew combative. I mistook their resistance for intellectual stubbornness. So I pressed harder—better arguments, more evidence. And they . . ." He paused. "They let me go."

As he said this, we were passing an ancient stone wall running alongside the road—centuries old, the kind that had marked boundaries since medieval times. This one was larger than any we'd seen, maybe fifty meters long and five meters high, high enough that you couldn't see what was on the other side. Normally I would've been studying the architectural detail, the dimensions of the stones, how carefully they were cut. Now the wall just looked imposing. A boundary marker, yes, but more a barrier to passage. It felt like an echo of the rigid orthodoxy Franco had faced at the seminary. Not a protection but a barrier to seeing the horizon.

"That must have been humiliating."

"It was."

"So what did you do?"

"Actually, nothing. For a few months anyway." He paused. "It took me that long to figure out what I wanted to do next. I kept going back to my training—I'm a church historian, after all. And when you're looking at how to navigate institutional resistance, Francis keeps coming up. He was someone who challenged orthodoxy by living the truth rather than arguing it."

He glanced at me. "My rediscovery of Francis so captured me I became a Third Order Franciscan."

"Third Order—what is that?"

"It's something Francis himself created to accommodate lay people—families, workers, anyone who wanted to dedicate themselves to his way of life without joining a monastery." He paused. "And studying more about Francis while preparing to take my vows—that's when the idea of the book occurred to me."

"So what was the idea that captured you?"

"The jumping off point was—here are two men fighting with the Church in very different ways. One a simple friar with no formal education, the other a Jesuit philosopher. Yet both arriving at the same insight. But as I got deeper into it, I realized the big idea was that God's love draws us forward, doesn't push from behind. That our contributions actually matter—we're participants, not spectators. The universe is still a work in progress, and what we do changes things. That reality is far less about who we are than what we are becoming."

Franco let that sit, eyes on the road.

Far less about who we are than what we are becoming. A very big idea.

I wanted to push back—or at least test it against something that had been bothering me since the train.

"I met someone on the train to Florence," I said. "An investment banker named David. We got into it about God and suffering—the usual questions. He'd grown up Jewish but said the only tenable position after the Holocaust is atheism—or at least giving up on the kind of God that Jews and Christians talk about. But he pushed harder than most. His nephew died at fourteen months from some rare genetic disorder. Seizures, feeding tubes, the whole nightmare. Good parents, faithful people, praying every night." I paused. "He asked me who he's supposed to blame for that. Not Hitler—he can't blame Hitler. But childhood leukemia? Earthquakes? The whole system?"

Franco was quiet for a moment. Then: "And what did you say?"

"I said maybe God suffers with us. That God is in it somehow, not above it controlling things." I shook my head. "He called it 'tragedy with company.' Said if that's the best God can do—suffer alongside—it's not a God worth worshiping."

"And you didn't have an answer."

"No. I still don't."

Franco nodded slowly, navigating a curve. "The God your friend is rejecting—the one who could stop a child's suffering but doesn't—that God deserves to be rejected. That's Zeus with better theology. A king on a throne who could intervene but chooses not to. Most people who reject God are rejecting that God." He glanced at me. "And they're right. That God is morally incoherent."

I hadn't expected that. "So you agree with him?"

"I agree with his rejection. Not his conclusion." Franco paused. "There's a word—panentheism. Not pantheism, where God equals everything. Panentheism. It means God is *in* everything, and everything exists *within* God. Not watching from outside. Not a spectator who could intervene but doesn't. Present within every part of creation, affected by what happens, feeling what it feels."

"But still not stopping the suffering."

"Because that's not how love works—not at any scale. Love doesn't coerce. It can't, or it isn't love. And if God *is* love, all the way down, then God can't override the freedom built into creation without ceasing to be God."

"Freedom," I repeated. "David would say his nephew didn't have freedom. A genetic mutation isn't a choice."

"No. But here's what Teilhard saw—the universe itself has something like freedom at every level. Not conscious choice, not moral agency, but genuine openness. Indeterminacy. From quantum events up to weather systems, tectonic plates, genetic mutations—reality isn't a machine God controls. It's alive, responsive, capable of going this way or that. God is in relationship with all of it, luring it toward love. But God can't coerce a cell any more than God can coerce a person. Not without destroying what makes it real."

I sat with that. Outside, the hills rolled past—ancient, indifferent, beautiful.

"So you're saying the earthquake that kills a quarter million people—God didn't send it, couldn't stop it, but was . . . in it somehow?"

"In the plates shifting. In the people running. In the ones who didn't make it out, and the ones who pulled survivors from rubble." Franco's voice was quiet. "Not causing it. Not watching it. *In* it. Grieving it. Working with whatever's left toward whatever healing is still possible."

"That's not much comfort to the dead."

"No. It isn't." He didn't try to soften it. "But it's a different question than the one your friend asked. He asked why an all-powerful God doesn't stop suffering. The answer is: that God doesn't exist. The God who *does* exist—if there is one—isn't all-powerful in that sense. This God is all-present. All-feeling. Working in and through everything, at every scale, with whatever agency will cooperate. But never forcing. Never overriding. That's the only way love can operate."

We drove in silence for a minute. I wasn't sure if I believed it. But for the first time since the train, I felt like I was hearing something that didn't insult the question.

"Tragedy with company," I said finally. "Maybe David was half right. Maybe that's all there is. But maybe . . . company isn't nothing."

"It isn't nothing," Franco said quietly. "It might be everything. When you're in the hospital with a dying child, you don't want explanations. You want someone to sit with you in the dark. If that's what God actually is—the presence that never leaves, the one who feels every loss—" He paused. "It's not an answer. But it might be the only honest place to stand."

This guy was already starting to feel like an old friend, even though this was only my second conversation with him.

"So after all that—the seminary, the book project, Francis—you ended up here? Driving pilgrims around Umbria?"

He shrugged. "I realized I'd spent too many years in libraries. If I wanted to understand what Francis actually discovered, I needed to be around people who were searching, not scholars who thought they'd already found the answers." He glanced at me. "Pilgrims like you. That's where the real theology happens."

We crested a hill, and suddenly Gubbio appeared below us—a medieval town climbing the lower slopes of Monte Ingino, stone buildings stacked against the hillside like steps.

"There it is," Franco said. "This is where Francis met the wolf."

"The wolf?"

"You don't know that story?" He seemed genuinely surprised. "It's one of the most famous. And it happened right here."

"I know bits and pieces. A wolf was terrorizing the town, Francis talked to it, everyone lived happily ever after. Something like that?"

Franco laughed. "Something like that. But the details matter." He slowed the van as we began the descent toward the walls. "This was maybe five years after Francis started his movement. The wolf had been killing livestock, then pets, then people. The townspeople were terrified. They'd sent out hunting parties, armed men—all the usual responses to threat. Nothing worked. The wolf kept killing."

"So they called in Francis?"

"They were desperate. And Francis did something nobody expected. He walked out to meet the wolf. Alone. Unarmed."

"That sounds insane."

"It does. But here's what interests me about the story—what Francis saw that nobody else could see. The hunting parties saw a monster, a threat to be eliminated. Francis saw something different."

"What?"

"Hunger." Franco let the word sit for a moment. "The wolf wasn't evil. It wasn't malicious. It was starving. And fear had made the townspeople incapable of seeing that. All they could see was threat. So they responded with force, which only made the wolf more desperate, more dangerous. A cycle of fear and violence that couldn't be broken because nobody could see what was actually driving it."

We passed through the city gate, the van's mirrors nearly brushing the ancient stone. The streets narrowed.

"What did Francis do?"

"He made a deal. He told the townspeople—if you agree to feed this wolf, it will stop killing. They thought he was crazy. But they were out of options, so they agreed. And it worked. The wolf lived peacefully in Gubbio for two more years. When it died, they buried it with honor."

I sat with that for a moment. "So the solution was that simple? Just feed it?"

"The solution was simple. Seeing it was hard." Franco pulled into a small piazza and turned off the engine. "That's what I keep coming back to. The townspeople weren't stupid. They weren't cruel. But fear had distorted their reasoning. They couldn't see hunger because all they could see was threat. And as long as they saw threat, their only response was more weapons, more hunting parties, more violence. Which only made things worse."

He turned to face me. "That's what I failed to understand at the seminary. My colleagues weren't being illogical or narrow-minded. They were brilliant scholars. But they were afraid. Teilhard's vision of an unfinished universe threatened something they needed to believe. And I couldn't see their fear because I was too busy being right."

"So you were like the hunting parties."

"Exactly. I saw threat—their narrow theology, their resistance to new ideas. So I attacked with better arguments, more evidence. All weapons. And the more I attacked, the more they defended. A cycle I couldn't break because I couldn't see what was actually driving it."

"Their hunger for certainty."

"Yes. Or their fear of losing it. Same thing, really." He paused. "Francis called this approach strategic innocence—seeing hunger instead of threat. Approaching without weapons. Not because you're naive about the danger, but because you understand that weapons only escalate the cycle."

"Strategic innocence," I repeated.

"It's not passivity. Francis still confronted the wolf. He still walked into danger. But he approached with curiosity instead of aggression. He wanted to understand what the wolf actually needed, not just eliminate the problem." Franco opened his door. "That's what I'm still learning. Eight years later, still learning."

I grabbed my pack from the back. "So with Wilhelm . . ."

"With Wilhelm, maybe ask yourself: is he mean, or is he hungry? Is he attacking you, or is he afraid of something?" Franco smiled. "Your collapse yesterday might have threatened something he needs to believe—that with enough preparation, enough discipline, failure is preventable. If you can see that hunger instead of just his sharpness, you might find he's less threatening than he seems."

We stood in the piazza, the medieval town rising around us.

"Franco, thank you. For the ride. For . . . all of this."

"For thinking out loud?" He shrugged. "That's what pilgrims are for, I'm discovering. Helps me figure out what I actually think." He paused. "Your friends should arrive mid-afternoon. Rest. Explore. And maybe—just maybe—when Wilhelm shows up tired from the trail, see if you can spot what he's hungry for instead of how he made you feel."

"Is he mean or is he hungry?"

"Exactly." Franco smiled. "Francis learned that lesson right here in this town. Maybe you will too."

I watched his van disappear into the medieval maze of streets, Franco's question still hanging in the air. Is he mean or is he hungry?

Somewhere in this town, eight centuries ago, a wolf had stopped killing because someone finally saw what it needed. I wondered if I could learn to see that clearly.

I checked into the hotel and dropped my pack. The guys wouldn't arrive until late afternoon. Time to rest, explore the city, let Franco's words settle.

The afternoon passed quietly. I walked Gubbio's ancient streets, found a cafe for lunch, sat with a coffee watching the piazza fill and empty. Franco's question kept circling back: *Is he mean or is he hungry?* I thought about Wilhelm at breakfast—his coffee untouched, his map folded with such precision. What was he protecting?

By late afternoon I was back at the hotel when I heard familiar voices in the plaza below. I looked out the window and saw them—Wilhelm, Thomas, Gunter, packs on their backs, tired but triumphant.

I went down to meet them.

"You made it!" Gunter called out, grinning as he dropped his pack.

"How was the hike?"

"Long," Wilhelm said. "But we finished together."

"Well, not all of us," I said with an openhanded shrug. "But I was really grateful for the break."

We found a small trattoria near the main square. The evening was warm, and they'd set tables outside in a courtyard lit by strings of lights. We ordered wine and pasta, and the guys told stories from their day on the trail—the steep sections, the views.

When there was a lull, I said, "Franco told me something interesting about Francis and the wolf of Gubbio. The way he framed it was different from what I'd heard before—not about taming a beast, but about seeing its hunger."

"The famous legend," Wilhelm said, stifling a yawn. "I've always found it a bit . . . fanciful."

"Maybe. But Franco's point wasn't really about the wolf." I paused, but I could see they were fading. Fifteen kilometers on the trail will do that. "It was about what becomes possible when you stop seeing threat and start seeing need."

Thomas nodded politely. Gunter was focused on his pasta. Wilhelm glanced at his watch.

"Anyway," I said, "something to think about. Maybe we can talk more tomorrow."

"Tomorrow," Gunter agreed, raising his glass. "When we're not half asleep."

We paid the bill and walked back through Gubbio's quiet streets. Tomorrow we would hike together to Biscina. But tonight, we were all ready for bed.

As we reached the hotel, a dog emerged from a doorway—someone's watchful pet. Pointed snout, angular ears, that old silhouette. It watched us pass, neither afraid nor aggressive. Just watching.

The Hunger Between Us

Tuesday morning, I woke to sunlight streaming through the windows of our Gubbio hotel. The medieval city was already stirring—bells from somewhere up the hillside, voices in the street below, the smell of espresso drifting up from the lobby.

I felt surprisingly good. The rest day had done its job. My knee was tender but not throbbing, and I was actually looking forward to exploring the city with the Germans.

When Gunter and I got down to the lobby, Wilhelm and Thomas were already halfway through breakfast.

"Jonathan! Looks like you're joining us today," Thomas said with a smile.

"I am indeed. Fairly confident we won't have a replay of day one."

Wilhelm gave me a friendly but skeptical look. "Let's hope."

Wilhelm pulled out his guidebook and spread it on the table between us. "Our hiking trail today is just fifteen kilometers. Generally downhill, just a few climbs, nothing too challenging."

"That sounds encouraging," I said.

"But," Wilhelm continued, and the others looked up, "because it's so short, we've got time to do some exploring here in Gubbio first. The city has far more interesting history than where we'll be staying tonight—an agriturismo in the middle of nowhere."

"How far up does the city go?"

"It climbs the hillside in tiers," Wilhelm said, tracing the route with his finger. "Stone houses, narrow streets, everything stacked one above the other. The Palazzo dei Consoli is about halfway up—maybe 150 meters elevation from here. Good resting place. Then the Basilica of Sant'Ubaldo at the summit." He looked at me. "We don't have to do the whole thing."

"Let's see how it goes," I said, trying to sound more confident than I felt.

No sooner had we dropped our napkins on the table than Wilhelm was out the front door, expecting us to be in tow.

We started up the narrow cobblestone streets, and for the first twenty minutes I felt good. Really good. I was keeping pace easily, even making conversation with Gunter about Franco's insights from yesterday.

The cobblestones were slick in places, uneven everywhere, and the streets switched back and forth through the compressed medieval layout. But I was managing fine. My knee wasn't bothering me at all—apparently, what I'd gotten was more of an abrasion and a bruise than anything serious. Maybe I'd worried too much about that.

Then, on the final approach to the Palazzo, things shifted. My breathing got heavier—not my knee, just the effort of hauling my weight up the hill. I didn't say anything, just kept climbing, thinking: if I can just make it to the Palazzo, maybe it'll be okay.

It struck me as odd, in hindsight, how much attention I'd given to the water situation on day one—counting bottles, rationing sips, calculating distances to the next spring. That was fixable. Add more bottles, drink more often, problem solved. But the weight I was carrying—the extra pounds I'd been meaning to lose for years—that required a kind of change I'd been avoiding. Funny how our attention gets drawn to the things we can actually address rather than the things that matter most. The doable rather than the important.

After another ten minutes, the Palazzo dei Consoli came fully into view—a Gothic sentinel perched on massive stone vaults, its bell tower watching over the valley. We reached the plaza in front of it, and I gratefully settled against the chest-high wall that bordered the edge.

I noticed the iron spikes covering the top of the wall. "That seems like overkill just to keep the birds off," I said to no one in particular.

Thomas glanced at them. "Probably says less about birds than about keeping people from crawling over."

"Fair point," I said, thinking about medieval defenses.

"The view from here is incredible," I added, genuinely meaning it. The whole valley spread out below us, terraced vineyards catching the late morning light.

Wilhelm consulted his guidebook, then looked up at us. "It's just another fifteen minutes if we get started now. Who's game?"

We all looked at each other. I was the first to speak.

"Not me. I'm gonna give it a rest here."

"Me too," Thomas said. I couldn't tell if he was doing it to be kind or trying to save his legs for later in the day.

"Make it three," Gunter added.

"No, no," I protested. "You guys don't hang back for me."

Gunter smiled, looked at Thomas and Wilhelm, then back at me. "I'm saving my feet. I don't want a recurrence of that first day's blister."

Wilhelm shrugged good-naturedly. "Suit yourselves. I'll meet you back at the hotel in an hour."

"I can't keep up with him," I said, watching Wilhelm disappear around the corner at a surprisingly quick pace. "But I sure admire his fortitude."

Gunter nodded. "Yeah, when we do Alpine hiking back home, he has the saying—'if you don't climb the mountain, the mountain will climb you.'"

We leaned against the waist-high spiked wall, looking out over the panorama of the city falling away beneath us—terraced houses, narrow streets, tile roofs catching the late light.

"These medieval buildings are charming," I said. "But I'll bet those houses are very uncomfortable to live in. Leaky, drafty, lots of holes to be patched."

Thomas looked at all of us and said, "Much like we are, guys."

Gunter let out a laugh. "Speak for yourself, Thomas. I'm not ready to concede yet."

"Would passing gas be considered leaky or drafty?" I asked.

Thomas groaned. Gunter just shook his head, grinning, and said, "I guess it depends on how much gas it is."

"I guess under the right circumstances middle school humor can still work." I decided not to add to the joke by making some comment about which end the gas escapes from.

We stood there in comfortable silence for a while. The wind that had been still in the streets below reached us here, carrying the sound of a distant bell—from the basilica further up the mountain where Wilhelm was headed.

When we felt like we had seen enough, the three of us headed down the mountain at a leisurely stroll, taking more time to look at the shops on the way. We beat Wilhelm back to the hotel, with him showing up about fifteen minutes after we did. We were having coffee at an adjacent trattoria when he walked up, the wet patches on his shirt showing just how much effort it had taken. He lowered himself into the open chair at our table with the careful movements of someone whose knees were protesting. Apparently, he did have his limits as well.

We paid for our coffees and headed back to the hotel to grab our day packs and walking sticks. The farmers market in the lower town square—earlier just a few people hanging up clothes and taking crates out of trucks, setting up tables—was now in full swing. The most entertaining part was watching a vendor wrestle live chickens out of wooden crates and tie their legs together with twine so buyers could carry them home upside down.

The unflappable calm of the man was quite a contrast to the hysterical chickens.

"He must've done that a thousand times," I suggested.

"I thought once their legs were tied they would continue to protest," I continued, "but apparently once bound and held upside down they actually calmed down."

"Not entirely calm," Gunter observed.

"I guess they sense the inevitable?" I said.

Wilhelm looked at us, not quite sure why we found it all so funny. "It's just the blood rushing into their heads." Then, unexpectedly, he added, "I wonder if someone held me upside down by my feet, it would calm me down like that."

We all looked at each other. Gunter grinned. "Maybe we should try and see?"

Thomas laughed, pointed his sticks toward the trail, and said, "Come on, pranksters. Biscina awaits."

The trail led us down from Gubbio's terraced heights, through olive groves that were just starting to show their silver-green leaves in the late morning light. For the first hour, we walked mostly in comfortable silence, finding our rhythm. My knee held. The pack felt manageable. Wilhelm set a steady pace—not too fast, not coddling either. Just the right speed for companions walking together.

Around mid-morning, we stopped at a spring beside the trail. The water was cold and clear, flowing from a carved stone fountain that had probably served pilgrims for centuries.

As we refilled our bottles, Wilhelm sat on the low wall surrounding the spring. He looked at me, then at Thomas and Gunter.

"I've been thinking," he said quietly, "about Franco's wolf story. About approaching without weapons."

We waited.

"It's harder than it sounds." As Wilhelm said this he was already standing and shouldering his pack so we could get started again, as though his comment didn't need to be addressed.

We fell into step behind him, the trail narrowing so we walked two by two. I found myself beside Gunter, with Wilhelm and Thomas ahead.

"I think that may be what's going on with my youngest son Heinric," Gunter said, thinking out loud. "Maybe he's not rejecting my advice. Maybe he's just . . . hungry for something else. To be seen as an adult, perhaps."

"Could be," I said. "I've been wondering the same thing about my evangelical friends. What if I've been so busy attacking their beliefs that I missed what they're actually hungry for?"

Thomas nodded. "I spend half my practice trying to help couples see this. And even when they get it intellectually, the next argument they're right back in the trenches. It's humbling how little insight actually changes behavior."

"That's the thing," Gunter said. "Even if I'm right about Klaus, I'm not sure I'd know how to do it differently. Old habits."

Wilhelm stopped and turned around.

"You gents have no idea how hard this actually is."

We caught up to him. His face wasn't angry—just tired. Realistic.

"My daughter tells me I make conversations feel like engineering problems. That I'm always trying to fix her instead of hearing her." He started walking again, slower now. "You think I haven't tried listening? You think I haven't tried not defending?"

None of us spoke.

"I know the theory. I've read the books. I've sat in the counselor's office with my wife, hearing all about how I need to be less rigid, more open, more vulnerable."

Thomas took note of the comment. If Wilhelm and his wife had taken those steps, they'd had some significant struggles. "How's that been for you?" he asked gently.

Wilhelm adjusted his pack straps. "I try. I genuinely try. I still do. And then she says something that feels like an attack, and before I can stop myself, I'm defending. Explaining. Proving my case."

He was quiet for a moment, as if realizing he'd said more than he meant to.

"Anyway. My point is—it's not simple."

The trail widened and we walked four abreast.

Gunter spoke quietly. "I wasn't trying to make it sound simple. I don't think it is."

"It's not," Wilhelm said. "That's my point. 'See their hunger instead of their threat'—it's a beautiful idea. But when you're in the moment, when someone you love is pushing every button you have, beautiful ideas don't help much."

He was quiet for a moment, then added: "And there's something else Franco's story doesn't address. That wolf was hungry. Fine. But some wolves are rabid. Some you can't negotiate with, can't feed into peace. They're not hungry—they're bent on destruction."

Thomas glanced at him. "You're thinking of something specific."

Wilhelm's jaw tightened. "I'm German. I'm always thinking of something specific." He didn't elaborate, but he didn't need to. The weight of his country's history was in the silence that followed.

"There's a verse," Wilhelm continued, his voice flatter now. "Jesus talking about the enemy. 'The thief comes only to steal and kill and destroy.' Some threats aren't misunderstood hunger. Some people—some systems—they just want to destroy. And all the strategic innocence in the world won't change that."

I thought of David on the train. His grandfather who spoke five languages. The educated men who built the camps. Knowledge hadn't saved anyone. Understanding hadn't either.

"So what do you do then?" Gunter asked quietly.

Wilhelm shook his head. "I don't know. That's my point. Franco's wolf story is beautiful. But it's not the whole story. Sometimes the wolf is rabid, and the only thing that stops it is a bullet."

The trail narrowed and we walked single file for a while, each of us alone with the weight of what he'd said.

When the path widened again, I finally asked, "So what does help?"

Wilhelm shook his head. "I don't know. That's what I'm saying. I've been trying for years with my daughter. With my wife. And I still get it wrong more than I get it right."

Thomas spoke carefully. "The people who make progress aren't those who think they have it figured out. They have the patience to keep showing up. To keep trying."

"Small comfort," Wilhelm said. But there was a slight softening in his voice.

We stopped for lunch at a small clearing with a view of the valley. Bread, cheese, some dried meat from our packs. We ate in silence for a while, the conversation still settling.

"The hunger between us," Thomas said quietly. "Maybe that includes the hunger to have easy answers."

Wilhelm nodded slowly. "And the hunger to fix things. To make them work properly." He looked at us. "That's my hunger. I see a problem, I want to solve it. Even when the problem is me."

We sat with that for a moment. Then we packed up and continued on.

We walked another hour or so after lunch, the talk of hunger and defenselessness settling into something quieter. The valley spread out beside us, calming in its indifference to our struggles. I found myself feeling something unexpected—not that we'd figured anything out, but that we were pointed in the right direction. We had the will, even if we hadn't yet found the way.

The agriturismo appeared in the distance—a cluster of stone farmhouses on a hillside, with the ruins of Biscina Castle rising behind them. The kind of place you could easily miss if you weren't looking for it.

"There," Gunter said, pointing. "Maybe thirty more minutes."

We made it in twenty-five.

The Tenuta di Biscina was a working farm—olive groves, livestock, fields of grain spreading across the hillside. The main building had been restored but kept its ancient bones, thick stone walls that would stay cool even in summer. From the terrace you could see across the valley to Monte Subasio, and I realized with a start that Assisi was just on the other side of that mountain.

As we checked in, the woman at the desk—Lucia, we'd learn—smiled at our dusty, tired group.

"Bene, bene," she said approvingly. "You walk from Gubbio today?"

"Si," Thomas replied in his careful Italian.

"Lungo cammino," she said. Long walk.

I looked at the others and said, "A good walk." They smiled and nodded, the kind of silent agreement that needs no translation.

That evening, we made our way to the agriturismo's restaurant—a simple dining room with a handful of tables, windows looking out over the valley. Most of the other guests were families on holiday, the children tired from the pool, the parents grateful for wine. We claimed a table by the window.

There was no menu. Lucia's husband brought out whatever they'd prepared that day—antipasti, then pasta, then meat with roasted vegetables, bread throughout, carafes of local red wine. The kind of meal where you stop keeping track of courses and just let it happen.

The mood was different than the heavy talk on the trail. Lighter. Something had been processed, and now we could just be companions sharing a meal.

"To Brother Wolf," Gunter said, raising his glass. "Who taught us something today."

We clinked glasses.

"So," Wilhelm said, pulling out his guidebook—of course he had his guidebook—"tomorrow. Valfabbrica. About eighteen kilometers, a bit more climbing than today."

"And the day after?" I asked.

"Assisi." Wilhelm looked up. "We'll be able to see it from the trail tomorrow afternoon. The basilica on the hill."

"I'm looking forward to finally seeing where it all started," I said.

Thomas nodded. "The place where a merchant's son became a saint."

Gunter leaned back in his chair. "You know what I'm looking forward to? Just sitting in that basilica. Not thinking. Not analyzing. Just being there."

Wilhelm smiled—a rare, unguarded smile. "That might be harder for some of us than others."

We laughed, and Lucia appeared with more wine.

"Piano, piano," she said, gesturing for us to slow down, enjoy. "La vita è bella."

Life is beautiful. Sitting here in a tiny agriturismo in the Umbrian hills, it was hard to argue with that. Surrounded by companions who had become something more than hiking partners—that was beauty enough for any day.

We lingered at the table as the other guests drifted off to their rooms, talking about nothing in particular—favorite meals from the trip so far, blisters and sore muscles, what we missed from home and what we didn't.

Eventually, we said our goodnights and headed to our rooms.

As I prepared for bed, part of me felt the familiar anxiety about tomorrow. Could I keep up? Would my knee hold? But something had changed. I wasn't thinking about it as a test to pass or fail anymore. I was just looking forward to walking with them, to finding value in whatever happened to emerge.

Lying there in the darkness, I realized something else: this whole pilgrimage wasn't teaching me to argue better or think more clearly. It was teaching me that connection comes before correction. That you can't have meaningful communication without trust, and you can't build trust while you're defending positions. All those years I'd spent perfecting my arguments for a better theology—maybe I'd been holding weapons the whole time, wondering why people kept seeing me as a threat.

But Wilhelm's words stayed with me too. Some wolves are rabid. Some threats aren't misunderstood hunger. I thought again of David on the train, his grandfather who spoke five languages, the educated men who understood perfectly and chose destruction anyway. Franco's wisdom was real—but it wasn't the whole story. Some darkness doesn't yield to understanding. Some evil isn't hungry; it's just evil.

I didn't know what to do with that. Maybe no one does.

I fell asleep thinking about hunger—mine, my companions', the wolf's, my evangelical friends'. And how different the world looks when you stop seeing threat and start seeing need. But also how dangerous it is to assume every threat is just hunger in disguise.

As I drifted off, the song returned. A new verse was forming around the idea of how fear distorts what we can see:

I know sometimes it seems unclear, but look again without your fear. Open your eyes and dry your tears, see what is arising.

Act III: The Franciscan Inversion

"No eye has seen, nor ear heard, nor the human heart conceived, what God has prepared for those who love him."

—1 Corinthians 2:9

"We are not going to change the world by attacking it or by repudiating it, but by reconnecting with the sacred matrix out of which we were born."

—Pierre Teilhard de Chardin

Speaking in Other Tongues

Wednesday morning, I woke early at the Biscina agriturismo. Gunter was already up in the other bed, dressed and putting on athletic shoes instead of his boots.

"Not your boots today?" I asked.

He grimaced slightly. "Serious blister I'm nursing. Need softer shoes for the day."

I dressed and packed quietly while he finished getting ready, then we went downstairs where Wilhelm and Thomas were having breakfast.

"Franco's picking me up this morning," I said as I sat down. "My knee did fine yesterday, but I'd rather not push it on back-to-back days."

Gunter glanced at his feet. "I'm a little bit jealous. You may have a much better day than I will."

"Toe still bothering you?" Thomas asked.

Gunter gestured to his shoes. "Bandaged and wrapped, cushioned shoe. It will be much better than yesterday."

"You're sure about riding instead of walking?" Wilhelm asked me.

"My knee held up yesterday, but fifteen kilometers was enough to remind me I'm not twenty anymore," I said. "I'll meet you in Valfabbrica."

We finished breakfast together, then said our goodbyes at the door—handshakes that felt warmer than they would have a few days ago. They shouldered their packs and headed out, and I waited.

About twenty minutes later, Franco's van pulled up. I tossed my pack in the back and climbed into the passenger seat.

"Buongiorno, Jonathan," he said, pulling onto the road. "How was yesterday's walk?"

"Good," I said. "Better than I expected, actually. My knee held. And the Germans—we had some real conversations. About the wolf story, about what it means to listen instead of fix."

Franco nodded, navigating the narrow road past the ruins of Biscina Castle.

I looked out at the Umbrian countryside rolling past. "I keep thinking about what you said. About Francis approaching the wolf without weapons. About seeing hunger instead of threat."

"And?" Franco asked.

"I'm not sure. Maybe it's starting to make sense. Or maybe I just want it to make sense."

Franco was quiet for a long moment, navigating a series of curves. Then he pulled the van over at a scenic overlook and turned to face me.

"Jonathan, what you've discovered—this is good. This clearing away of defensive ego, this learning to be present without weapons—it's essential. You've done the work of understanding it. Now you must learn to tune out the ego noise. Only then can begin to see like Francis."

He held up a hand, smiling. "But there's more. What you've learned gives you the foundation, the posture, the cleared space. But now you need the art."

"The art?"

"The art of communication. The art of actually hearing what people are saying beneath what they're saying. The art of speaking in other tongues."

I must have looked confused because Franco laughed. "Don't worry—this is the good part. You've done the hard work of becoming available, of learning presence. Now I get to show you what becomes possible from that cleared space. Think of it like this: you've learned to stop defending yourself. That's crucial. But now—what do you do with that openness? How do you actually use it to build bridges?"

"Tell me," I said, and I meant it. This didn't feel like another burden, another layer of complexity I was getting wrong. It felt like Franco was about to hand me a tool I'd been needing.

"Okay," Franco said, pulling back onto the road. "So yesterday you had that conversation about the wolf, about seeing hunger instead of threat. That's beautiful. That's the foundation. But let me ask you something—when your evangelical friends talk about biblical authority or sexual purity, what do you hear?"

I thought about it. "Honestly? I hear fear. Rigidity. People clinging to certainty because they're afraid of uncertainty."

"Exactly," Franco said. "You hear threat. Or you hear ignorance. But what if they're speaking a language you've forgotten how to understand? What if they're not just defending propositions—what if they're speaking from an entirely different orientation about what matters?"

"I'm listening."

"There's a psychologist named Jonathan Haidt who studies moral foundations—the basic orientations people have about what's important, what's sacred, what needs protecting. He identifies several: care, fairness, loyalty, authority, sanctity, liberty. Different people weight these differently. It's like having different primary colors in your moral palette."

"So progressives and conservatives aren't just disagreeing about conclusions," I said slowly. "They're starting from different foundations entirely."

"Exactly!" Franco's enthusiasm matched mine now. "Your progressive friends speak the language of care and fairness and liberty. But your evangelical friends? Many of them speak the language of sanctity and authority. They're oriented around what's sacred, what's holy, what needs to be set apart and protected."

"So when they talk about sexual purity . . ."

"They're not just being repressive. They're speaking from a sanctity orientation. They're trying to protect something they experience as sacred. And you—speaking from a care and liberty orientation—hear 'purity' and translate it as 'shame and control.' But they're saying something completely different."

"This is why the wolf story resonated," I said. "Seeing hunger instead of threat. But you're giving me a way to understand what they're actually hungry for."

"Yes! And from the cleared space you've created—from that place of not defending yourself—you can actually hear it. When you're not busy protecting your own position, you have the capacity to recognize: oh, this person is speaking from sanctity. They're trying to protect sacred space. I don't have to share that orientation to respect it."

"Give me an example," I said. "Something concrete."

Franco thought for a moment. "Okay. Francis and Clare. You know this story?"

"A little."

"Clare was young, beautiful, from a wealthy, noble family. She could have had any life she wanted. Instead, she left everything to follow Francis's vision. And they had this incredibly intimate relationship—spiritual partners for decades. But it was chaste."

"Chaste. That's a word you don't hear much anymore." Wondering, I asked, "Did people think they were sleeping together? I mean by this time he was pretty seriously famous right, maybe people trusted him?"

"Those who knew him, yes, of course. But many probably saw Francis as repressed, maybe afraid of his desire, possibly psychologically damaged—all the usual modern assumptions," Franco offered. "But what if their chastity wasn't about repression at all? What if it was about consecration? About setting something apart as so valuable that directing it differently might create space for a different kind of intimacy?"

I thought about that. "Intimacy without possession."

"Exactly. Clare wasn't Francis's property or his temptation. She was his equal, his companion, his mirror. Their choice to remain chaste wasn't fear—it was freedom. It was saying: this dimension of human connection is so valuable, we're going to consecrate it, set it apart, and see what other forms of knowing become available."

"That's the sanctity orientation," I said.

"Yes. And from your cleared space, from that place where you're not defending your progressive positions, you can actually hear it. You can understand: they're not damaged or backwards. They're speaking from a different moral foundation. They're oriented toward the sacred in a way you're not, and that's okay. You don't have to adopt their orientation to respect it. You don't have to agree with their applications to honor their hunger."

I thought about the celibate priest from our conversation before. "I want to hear more about your priest friend. How did he get from 'I don't want this' to actually finding it meaningful?

"What changed?"

"He stopped fighting it and started exploring what the space created by celibacy might offer. And you know what he discovered? He became a better friend. More present, more available, more genuinely curious about others. His colleagues—men and women both—started seeking him out not because he was trying to befriend them, but because he'd learned to listen without agenda."

"Without the constant background noise," I said.

"Exactly. He told me once that celibacy freed up enormous mental bandwidth. All that energy that usually goes into romantic strategizing, into thinking about relationships, into the whole dance of attraction and pursuit—it just became available for other things. For his teaching, for friendship, for actually being present to whatever was in front of him."

"And he's happy?"

"Genuinely happy. Not gritting his teeth through it—actually flourishing. Which doesn't mean everyone should be celibate," Franco added quickly. "But it means the sanctity orientation isn't just repressive nonsense. It's responding to something real about how humans can direct their energies, about what becomes possible when you consecrate something rather than consume it."

I thought about all the times I'd dismissed purity culture, saw abstinence as impractical thinking. "So when I was arguing against evangelical sexual ethics . . ."

"You were treating sanctity as the enemy instead of recognizing it as a different language. A different way of orienting toward what matters."

The road wound down through the valley, and I could see a village ahead—Valfabbrica, where we'd spend the night.

"Here's the thing," Franco said. "There's research suggesting that couples who delay sexual involvement report higher relationship satisfaction—not because sex is bad, but because they built other forms of intimacy first."

"So it's not about who's right," I said slowly. "It's about recognizing that different people are oriented toward different aspects of reality, and all of them might be seeing something true."

"Yes! And from the place you've reached—that cleared, non-defensive space—you can actually explore that. You can ask: what are they protecting? What do they hold sacred? What are they hungry for beneath their positions? Not so you can defeat them or convert them, but so you can actually hear them."

"It's like learning another language," I said.

"Exactly. Francis was multilingual in this deeper sense. He could speak the language of both celibacy and celebration. He knew both of the pull of wealth and the gift of poverty. He wasn't just good with words. He'd learned to recognize and respect different orientations, different ways of being oriented toward the sacred."

We were approaching Valfabbrica now, the medieval village clustered on a hillside ahead.

"There's a story," I said, "from just before I came on this pilgrimage. A sermon about Pentecost."

"Tell me," Franco said.

"The pastor talked about how when the Spirit showed up in Acts, everyone heard the apostles speaking in their own native language. And he pointed out that everyone in that crowd probably spoke Greek—it was the common language of the Empire. But the Spirit didn't just settle for a language everyone understood. It went further, translating the message into every dialect represented. Every person heard in their native tongue."

"The gift of tongues," Franco said quietly.

"Right. And the preacher's point was that you can have the most important truth in the world to communicate, but if you're not speaking in the language the person can actually hear—not just understand intellectually, but really hear in their bones—then real communication won't happen. The Spirit's gift wasn't uniformity. It was comprehension across diversity."

"The Spirit doesn't erase different dialects," Franco said. "It gives the ability to hear each other clearly despite them."

"And these moral orientations—sanctity, authority, care, liberty—they're like native languages. Most people only speak one or two fluently. But from a cleared space, from that place where you're not defending yourself, you can start to learn others. Not so you can become a native speaker, but so you can recognize when someone is speaking from sanctity instead of care, from authority instead of liberty."

Franco pulled into a small parking area near the pensione. Through the windshield, I could see the village's stone buildings, ancient and unpretentious.

"So the art of communication," I said, "isn't just about listening and being patient. It's about learning to recognize what moral foundation someone is speaking from, so you can actually hear what they're saying beneath their words."

"Yes," Franco said. "And more than that—it's about respecting those foundations even when you don't share them. You don't have to think sanctity is the most important value. But you have to grant that for some people, it is. And their hunger for the sacred, for the set-apart, for the consecrated—it's not ignorance or fear. It's a legitimate way of being in the world."

"Even if I think they're wrong about how they apply it?"

"Even then. Because once you respect the orientation itself, you can have real conversations about application. But as long as you're treating the orientation as something to be overcome or evolved past, you're not having a conversation. You're just waiting for them to become more like you."

I looked at the village. "And Francis figured this out."

"Francis lived this. He didn't just tolerate different orientations—he recognized the hunger in each one and found ways to speak to it. He could address the wealthy in the language of liberation, the poor in the language of dignity, the powerful in the language of humility, the humble in the language of worth. He became fluent in the full range of human hungers."

His words were resonating. This was a little intimidating but it made perfect sense.

He continued, "Your evangelical friends hear 'deconstruction' and think 'destruction of truth.' But if you spoke in their language, you might be able to help them hear 'reconstruction' or 'refinement' or 'deepening.' Same truth, different tongue."

Franco turned off the engine. "The others should arrive in a few hours. Get settled, rest your knee. Tomorrow we'll have time to explore what Francis discovered—Assisi is just over the mountain."

I climbed out, shouldering my pack, and looked at this quiet village where pilgrims had stopped for centuries. Somewhere over that ridge was Assisi, where a merchant's son had learned to speak in other tongues. Had learned to hear the hunger beneath the words. Had discovered that the cleared space of ego-death wasn't the end—it was the beginning of a whole new art.

"So all that work in Act Two," I said, "learning to be present, to see clearly, to put down my weapons—that was preparing me for this."

"Exactly," Franco said. "You can't learn another language while you're busy defending your own. But once you've cleared that space, once you've learned to listen without agenda—then the whole art of communication becomes possible."

He helped me carry my pack to the pensione entrance. "Rest well, Jonathan. Tomorrow we go to Assisi."

I watched him drive away, then turned to look at the hills. The afternoon sun was warm on the stone walls. In a few hours, the Germans would arrive, tired and triumphant from their walk. Tonight, we'd share a meal and stories. And tomorrow—tomorrow we'd finally see the city where it all began.

I felt hopeful in a way I hadn't in years—not the brittle hope of having the right answers, but the grounded hope of finally asking better questions. Questions like: What language are they speaking, and can I learn to hear it? What are they hungry for, and can I respect it even if I don't share it?

Breaking Ground

Dawn came slowly to Valfabbrica. I sat with my coffee in the pensione's courtyard, listening to the town stirring. The morning had that peculiar Italian quality where time seems to slow down, as if the day itself is taking a deep breath before beginning.

Franco's van pulled into the small plaza earlier than expected, and I could see him through the windshield, raising a coffee cup in greeting.

"Buongiorno, my friend," he called, climbing out with more energy than a man his age should have at this hour. "I have good news. I decided I would like to spend more time in Assisi, so I've dropped my other clients for the day. I'll be staying overnight with an old friend, which means we can explore properly—not just a quick drop-off."

Franco rarely deviated from his efficient porter routine. "What changed your mind?"

"Sometimes a place calls to you," he said with that enigmatic smile, but his eyes held something more intentional. "And sometimes you need to see through Francis's eyes before you can understand what he really discovered."

There was something deliberate in his tone. Franco had a way of seeing where I was headed before I did. He never lectured, but our conversations always seemed to be building toward something—layers of meaning accumulating like sediment until suddenly a new landscape was revealed.

As we wound up from the valley floor, the morning mist lifted from the Umbrian hills like a veil being drawn back.

"You know," Franco said, navigating a particularly sharp turn, "I've been driving pilgrims along this route for twenty years, and every time I make this ascent, I think about transformation—how gradually, then suddenly, everything changes."

"Like faith?" I asked.

"Like everything that matters. Evolution, consciousness, love—they all work the same way. Slow accumulation, then sudden emergence of something genuinely new."

Then, as we came over a rise, Assisi appeared. The city looked like it had grown straight out of the mountainside, its rose-colored walls so perfectly matched to the rock that you couldn't tell where nature ended and human work began.

The sight hit me with unexpected force—not just aesthetic appreciation, but something deeper. This was where Francis had grown up, where he'd started seeing things differently. Where a merchant's son had become a mystic who changed the world not through force but through a kind of radical openness.

"There's something about spring here—even the stones seem to be waking up after winter," Franco said, gesturing toward the walls where morning shadows crept and retreated, making the ancient stonework seem almost alive.

"When most people look at this, all they see are the stones—the fortress, the protection, the weight and permanence," Franco continued. "But what attracted Francis was always the life that moved in and around these heavy stones."

"The life within the structure," I said.

"More than that. Francis could actually imagine what Jesus meant when he said that if people fell silent, even the stones would cry out with glory to God. Not metaphorically—literally. From the simplest stone to the most complex creature, the life of God is at work in all of it, pushing toward greater complexity, greater consciousness, greater love."

Franco shifted the van into gear and we began the final descent toward the city gates. I rolled down the window, letting the cool morning air fill the van, carrying with it the scent of turned earth and new growth.

"Franco, you're sounding almost pantheistic—like God is everything."

He smiled. "You're close, but not quite. I don't believe God is everything. I believe his presence is within everything. It's called panentheism—important not to confuse those. That little 'en' from the Greek makes all the difference."

He paused, letting me process the distinction. "Pantheism says God *equals* the universe. Panentheism says the universe exists *within* God, while God also transcends it. Like a child in the womb—within the mother, dependent on her, but the mother is more than the child she carries.

"And if you follow that thought," he continued, warming to the topic, "it leads you to see the universe quite differently.

No longer as finished but as an ongoing creation. Not as something once perfect now broken, but as something that is still in process of becoming, still learning."

"When I lost my position over this, I told myself that my colleagues were just closed-minded old men protecting the accepted orthodoxy." He paused. Apparently seeing something down the road that I couldn't see. Now that I've had a few years to think about it, they sensed just how destabilizing Teilhard's ideas would be. Einstein had just blown Newton's clockwork cosmos apart—and here comes this Jesuit saying the same is true theologically. Creation isn't finished."

Why was that so threatening?"

"Because it implied that God was still creating. Even more radically it suggested he is learning in the process. It would undermine the reigning view for most of church history of a sovereign who has preordained everything."

"God learning? That really is a radical idea."

"And yet that not only aligns with the evidence of evolution but better explains all those stories in the old testament where God changes his mind..."

I finished his thought. "Because he learned something!"

"Ironically, they completely missed another of his core ideas, one very relevant to our discussions about AI. He called it the "noosphere". The integrated accumulation of and access to knowledge itself, the collective store of mankind's wisdom and imagination. With generative AI this notion moved from wholly abstract to actually conceivable."

"Because we might actually be watching it emerge?" I asked.

"That's a serious question that bears more discussion. But I don't think Teilhard would disagree."

He turned back to the question of God's power. "As fascinating as this noosphere idea is," he said. "I think it was his redefinition of the nature of God's power that was the larger problem. The idea that creation was not a finished project. Not as something that was perfect and fell, but as something that's still becoming, still emerging into greater complexity and consciousness."

These ideas resonated in a way I hadn't expected. What if the universe really was unfinished? What if AI offered a way to learn not just knowledge, but wisdom. What if it really does help see past our tribal biases? I would have to sits with these questions for a while.

"Franco, I have to be honest—I think I've exceeded my limit for big questions for today.

Franco offered a sympathetic grin I could imagine him using with his students in class.

"Just one more then we'll move on. It is Tielhard's idea of the universe being in process of complexification.

"Complexification? That sounds challenging but I'll give it a go. What exactly does that mean?"

"It is simply his term for the direction of evolution. Teilhard argued that everything is building toward greater complexity. Atoms become molecules, molecules become cells, cells to creatures, creatures become minds. And the more complex something gets, the more aware it becomes.

"OK, I get it. This does add another important piece to the puzzle."

He continued. "Complexification is key to understanding his work. He saw the universe not only as having positive direction and building toward greater complexity, but also that consciousness emerges from complexity."

"I am having difficulty understanding why that would be controversial. What's the problem?"

"The church said it contradicted scripture—Genesis taught that consciousness appeared in an instant with Adam and Eve. God breathed, man became a living soul. But what really upset them was the implied pantheism. If consciousness is present all the way down, if humans are on a continuum with animals and cells, what happens to the uniqueness of the soul?"

"So what was Teilhard saying?"

"That the breath was a catalyst—the tipping point when complexity had built to where a higher consciousness could emerge. The awareness you and I have has been growing since the first particles started forming relationships."

"I can see why that troubled them."

"Yes, it added the question of the nature of man to the question of how God's power is exercised." After letting that settle he continued. "The scientists had trouble with this idea as well. Physics had given us the law of entropy—all energy dissipates, systems run down. And here comes Teilhard saying there's another arrow. Complexity is increasing. Consciousness is accumulating."

"So both sides rejected him?" I hadn't known that. Franco nodded. "Initially yes. But he was not denying entropy. He was saying it's not the whole story."

"So two forces working at once—one winding down, one building up?"

"Exactly. And that's what made his claim so radical. Scientists saw pockets of complexity as temporary anomalies—local resistance to inevitable decay. Teilhard said the building is as fundamental as is the decay. Consciousness accumulating isn't an accident. It's what the universe is doing."

"And the scientists didn't like that?"

"To them it seemed foolish. Entropy was settled science, one of the most well-established laws in physics. The universe runs down. That's not a theory; that's what the data showed. Teilhard's idea didn't fit the paradigm. It sounded like wishful religious thinking dressed up in scientific language."

I thought about that. "Here's what I don't understand. If Teilhard was saying the universe is moving toward something— building, emerging into greater awareness—isn't that more aligned with the biblical narrative than entropy? A good God redeeming creation, drawing everything toward wholeness?"

Franco's eyes lit up. "Now you see the irony. The church rejected an idea that was fundamentally religious. A universe winding down to nothing isn't the biblical story. But a universe that is waking up, that is learning how to really love is. Teilhard offers us a coherent framework that is both deeply biblical and scientifically credible. I hope the church has the imagination and faith to see it."

"So where does that leave him now? What is the Catholic church's current view? Is he still on the outs? He seems to be based on your experience at the seminary."

Franco shook his head. "Yes, the conservatives still largely don't get him. Remember the church had outlawed his work during his lifetime. It was only after his death in 1955, when the friends he had given the manuscripts, ignored the church and began publishing all of his work."

"That was the year I was born. Actually both Steve Jobs and Bill Gates were born that year as well."

"Interesting. Apparently a good year for tech titans?" He said with a wink.

"Same year different league." I countered.

He continued. "The scientific community had found him easy to ignore, an obscure unpublished Jesuit philosopher talking about the moral direction of evolution wasn't worth engaging."

"What changed?"

"Two things. First, Vatican II. As the council thought through the church's relationship to the modern world, Teilhard's ideas didn't seem so foreign anymore. Around that time, in the scientific community they were discussing something they called complexity theory. Researchers had started asking how order arises from chaos, how systems self-organize. These were questions Teilhard had been asking decades earlier. Almost overnight they went from irrelevant to prescient."

"So what do you think Francis would have thought of Teilhard's views?"

Franco laughed softly.

"He wouldn't have understood a word of it. Noosphere? Complexification? Francis was no intellectual. But the essence of it—that creation is sacred, that everything is connected, that the universe is alive with the presence of God?" He nodded. "Francis knew that in his bones. He just didn't need the science to get there."

Franco pointed ahead through the windshield. "San Damiano is just around this bend. This is where it all began for him—where he first heard the voice that would change everything."

The road narrowed into a shaded lane. The lane curved gently upward, and as we emerged into a small parking area, I saw it—a simple stone church nestled against the hillside like it had grown there rather than been built.

The chapel was smaller than I'd expected, its honey-colored stone glowing in the morning light. We entered through a low doorway that forced us to duck slightly—a physical reminder of the humility required to enter sacred space.

Inside, the air was cool and still. Light filtered through small windows, creating pools of illumination that moved slowly across the ancient floor as the sun shifted. The space felt alive despite—or perhaps because of—its emptiness. A wooden cru-cifix hung on the far wall, simple and stark.

"This is where Francis heard the voice," Franco said softly. "He was praying here when the crucifix spoke to him: 'Francis, repair my church, which as you can see is falling into ruin.'"

I studied the cross, imagining a young merchant's son kneeling here, his world about to crack open.

"At first, he thought it meant this building," Franco continued. "So he started carrying stones, repairing the chapel himself. Only later did he understand it meant something larger—the whole church, the whole way of being Christian in the world."

We sat on a stone bench along the wall. The silence between us felt comfortable, expectant.

The idea was so vast I could barely hold it. Yet sitting in this simple chapel, it felt almost obvious—of course everything was connected, of course consciousness ran through everything, of course love was the force that moved the sun and stars, as Dante had written.

We sat in silence for a while, and I found myself doing something that would have surprised my younger self—I was praying, but not the way I'd been taught. There was no petition, no list of requests, no attempt to bend God's will toward my concerns. Instead, I was simply . . . present. Aligned. Listening for what was already emerging rather than asking for something new.

"Franco," I said quietly, "I think something's changed in how I pray."

He waited, knowing I needed to work it out.

"For fifty years, prayer meant asking—asking God to change circumstances, heal people, intervene in the world. Petition, supplication, intercession. The language of a subject addressing a sovereign." I paused, watching the light shift across the stone floor. "But these last two weeks, I've stopped asking God to do things and started . . . I don't know . . . consenting to what's already happening. Like prayer isn't about bending the divine will but aligning my heart with it."

Franco's eyes brightened. "You're discovering what the mystics have always known—that prayer is primarily ego-emptying, not petition. It's not about getting God to do what you want. It's about releasing your grip on what you think should happen so you can see what actually is happening."

"So prayer is . . . surrender?"

"Not quite. Surrender implies defeat. This is more like . . . clearing. Like a gardener clearing ground before planting. You're not giving up—you're removing the clutter so something can grow. Every time you pray without asking for anything, you're practicing that kind of clearing. Making space for emergence rather than demanding intervention."

I thought about all those years of prayer meetings, intercession lists, asking God to change outcomes. Had any of it worked the way we thought? Or had we been missing the point entirely?

"The moment you stop defending your agenda in prayer," Franco continued, "you can finally participate in what's actually unfolding. It's the same principle Francis discovered—powerlessness is power. Not because weakness is strong, but because only an empty hand can receive."

"But Franco," I said, sitting up straighter on the stone bench, "when evangelicals talk about love, they always rank them—eros is bodily passion, phileo is friendship, and agape is the highest form. God's perfect love, transcendent and pure. What you're describing sounds almost . . . material. Physical."

Franco's eyes lit up with that particular gleam I'd come to recognize when a theological puzzle piece was about to click into place. "Exactly! And that's the problem with how we've been taught agape for centuries. We made it so transcendent, so spiritual, so perfect that it became a prison—locked away from daily life. An ideal to aspire to but never actually touch."

He shifted on the bench, warming to the topic. "Think about the traditional hierarchy. Eros is bodily and suspect—something to be controlled or overcome. Phileo is relational and good—friendship, loyalty. But agape? Agape is spiritual and untouchable. God's love from the throne room of heaven. Beautiful theology. Useless for Tuesday morning."

"What do you mean?"

"I mean, what does that theology give you when your child is sick at 3 a.m. and you're exhausted and you show up anyway? When you persist in a difficult relationship not because you feel transcendent spiritual love but because you're committed?"

"I never thought about it that way."

"That's because we were taught to think agape was something else—something higher, something we could only aspire to. But what if we've had it backwards?" Franco gestured toward the cross on the wall. "What if agape isn't the most ethereal form of love but the most concrete? Not distant perfection but persistent presence?"

All this talk about love brought to mind someone I met at Wild Goose. "Franco, what you just said reminded me of a conversation I had with a theologian, Thomas Oord, at Wild Goose—this progressive Christian festival I went to just before coming on the pilgrimage. Oord told me he was working on a systematic theology of love and said something startling: no one had ever written one before. Is that true?"

"Thomas Oord," Franco said with recognition. "He's doing some pioneering work in open and relational theology. Yes, it does seem surprising, doesn't it? But he's right. It's just another example of how we imprisoned agape in transcendence. We made love so spiritual, so otherworldly, that it couldn't be the organizing principle for anything practical."

He turned back to face me. "But when you shift your understanding of God—from only transcendent to present within everything—suddenly agape gets liberated from that prison. It's not distant perfection anymore. It's the most material, daily, concrete thing there is."

"The force that holds everything together," I said, remembering his earlier words.

"Yes! The power that keeps showing up. The committed choice to stay present through difficulty. To persist in relationship when it would be easier to leave. To show up exhausted because someone needs you. That's agape. And it's not weak or ethereal—it's the strongest force in reality."

"And Francis understood this?"

"Francis lived it. He didn't have the theological language—he didn't need it. When he kissed the leper, he wasn't reaching for some distant spiritual ideal. The love didn't start with Francis's kiss. It was already present—surrounding that man, sustaining him, and now inviting Francis to stop running from it. He learned that agape must be incarnate to be effective—that was the foundation of Jesus' teaching."

"But here's what most people miss about Francis," Franco continued, his voice taking on a different intensity. "They think his poverty was the goal—that stripping naked in the square, giving away his inheritance, living with nothing was about poverty itself. But poverty wasn't the point. It was the mechanism."

"Mechanism for what?"

"For clearing ego. For removing every buffer between himself and the world's need." Franco leaned forward. "Think about it—every possession you own is a layer of protection from complexity, from relationship, from love's demand. Your money protects you from having to depend on others. Your status protects you from being dismissed. Your theological certainties protect you from having to sit with mystery."

"So Francis wasn't rejecting wealth—he was clearing obstacles?"

"Exactly. He discovered what the Eastern mystics call 'kenosis'—self-emptying. But he wasn't emptying himself because emptiness was holy. He was clearing space because only in that cleared space could love actually emerge. When you have nothing left to defend, you finally have the freedom to genuinely connect."

Franco gestured toward the simple stone walls around us. "This is why he loved places like San Damiano. Not because poverty is beautiful, but because simplicity creates conditions. No distractions, no protections, no buffers. Just you and the love that's trying to move through you toward others."

"It's like . . . ego-clearing creates the conditions where love can emerge?"

"Precisely. Love is always present, always moving. But the ego builds walls to protect itself—walls of possession, reputation, certainty, control. Francis found the fastest way to dismantle those walls: give away everything they were built to protect. Not as punishment, not as asceticism for its own sake, but as strategic clearing. The Franciscan inversion isn't about poverty. It's about removing every obstacle to love's emergence."

I thought about my own layers of protection—my theological sophistication, my writing platform, my reputation as someone who'd "thought through" faith. Were these helping me connect with others, or protecting me from having to risk genuine encounter?

"So when I'm clinging to being right about theology . . ."

"You're maintaining the buffer. Defending ego instead of clearing space." Franco smiled gently. "The pilgrimage isn't just about walking miles, Jonathan. It's about walking away from everything you use to protect yourself from genuine relationship. Every step that wears you down, makes you dependent on these three Germans you barely knew two weeks ago—that's ego-clearing. That's the Franciscan mechanism at work."

I sat with that for a moment, watching dust motes drift through the shaft of sunlight coming through the window. It made sense of something I'd been struggling with for years—the disconnect between the "highest form of love" I'd been taught about and the exhausting, daily work of actually loving people.

"So agape isn't the love we can't quite reach," I said slowly. "It's the love we're already doing—we just didn't recognize it because we'd been taught to look for something more . . . spiritual."

"More transcendent," Franco corrected gently. "But transcendence without immanence is just absence. God isn't only 'up there' or 'back then.' God is here, now, in the material world, and agape is how that presence moves—persistent, committed, staying-with. Not soft love. Strong love. The strongest there is."

Something clicked. "What you just said," I remarked. "It brought to mind that chapter in First Corinthians about love that everyone quotes at their weddings."

"Yes, it may be the most powerful poem in all of the New Testament," Franco said. "But to our point here, the passage ends by saying, 'Where there are prophecies, they will cease; where there is knowledge, it will pass away . . . And now these three remain: faith, hope, and love.'"

"Yes, and?" I said, not understanding exactly where he was going.

"After the prophecies and propositions have passed away, faith, hope, and love remain. All relational."

I let out a slow breath as it hit me. "How many times have I read that passage without seeing it?" I said, almost to myself. "How many other passages are sitting there like that—hiding huge things in plain sight?"

Franco nodded slowly. "This is one of the reasons the early church became comfortable with the odd, mind-expanding idea of the Trinity. God lives in relationship—not like an unapproachable sovereign, distant and singular. The Trinity isn't about counting—it's about relationship. God's very nature is relational flow, mutual indwelling, love exchanged."

"So within the Trinity itself," I said slowly, "God is experiencing faith, hope, and love?"

Franco's eyes lit up. "Yes! That's it exactly. Faith as trust between Father, Son, and Spirit. Hope as openness to what emerges in their relationship. Love as the bond itself, the mutual indwelling the early church called *perichoresis*—the divine dance."

"So when Paul says these three remain . . ."

"He's not just giving moral instruction. He's describing the eternal nature of God. The relational reality that was before creation and will be after everything else passes away."

As he said this, I felt the pieces falling into place. "He was trained in the Hebrew scriptures—stories of a God who argues with Abraham, wrestles with Jacob, makes and breaks and remakes covenants. Fundamentally relational and messy, not ordered propositions."

"Exactly. Paul's Hebrew heritage combined with his Greek education allowed him to reframe these fundamental insights. He came from a people whose entire theology was relational—a God who shows up, who responds, who stays faithful through relationship."

"Which means Open and Relational theology isn't a departure from scripture," I said. "It's a return to what Paul was saying all along."

I thought about all the battles over correct doctrine, over who's in and who's out. "The greatest of these is love—not because it's the most spiritual, but because it's the most fundamentally relational. It can't be corrupted into propositions the way faith and hope can."

"Exactly. Faith becomes 'believing the right things.' Hope becomes 'my personal salvation.' But love?" Franco spread his hands. "Love only exists in the doing, in the between. That's why it's greatest—it reveals what faith and hope truly are when they're held in relationship rather than reduced to individual certainties."

Franco leaned forward. "And Paul reinforces this elsewhere. 'The letter kills, but the Spirit gives life.' It's a fundamental thread running through everything he wrote—the limits of codes, creeds, laws."

Franco paused, studying me before saying, "It's not only theology—it's also in the stories. Take the book of Acts for an example. Who is the main character in the book of Acts?"

My mind immediately went to the old debate. "Peter starting the church or Paul expanding its boundaries? They're both good candidates." I shrugged. "Not sure."

"It's neither," Franco said.

"What do you mean? There are no characters more major than those two."

"What about the Holy Spirit?"

I stared at him. "The Holy Spirit?"

"Everything in that book starts with the Holy Spirit calling, the Holy Spirit nudging, the Holy Spirit voicing some truth that moved them forward. The Spirit is the main character of Acts— the motivating force inside every story being told there."

"So what do I do with this?" I asked.

Franco waited.

After what seemed like several minutes, I said, "Stop defending positions and start tending emergence. I guess, in a way, to learn to treat faith like Francis treated this chapel—not as something to argue about but as something to rebuild, stone by stone, with patience and presence."

Franco nodded. "Good. But remember—seeds don't argue the soil into growth. They simply unfold according to their nature when conditions are right. Your work isn't to force anything but to create conditions where new life can emerge."

"How do I do that?"

"The same way Francis did. Start with what's broken. Not to condemn it but to understand it. Then begin the slow work of rebuilding—not alone but in community, not through force but through invitation."

As we prepared to leave, Franco turned for one last look at the cross.

We walked back toward the van in companionable silence. The morning had grown warmer, and the air was filled with the sound of bees working the wildflowers that grew along the path. Everything seemed vibrantly alive, participating in some great work I was only beginning to perceive.

As Franco started the engine, he gave me that knowing look I'd come to recognize. "The ground has been broken, my friend. Now we wait to see what emerges."

"How long does that take?"

"As long as it takes. Francis worked on this chapel for two years. Teilhard spent his entire life developing his vision and died before it could be published. But the seeds they planted are still growing, still breaking ground in new places, still pushing toward light."

As we drove away from San Damiano, something inside me tilted—not dramatic, just a subtle reorientation, like a plant turning toward sun. The questions that had tormented me for years were still there, but they felt different now. Less like problems to be solved and more like seeds that had been planted, waiting for the right season to break through into light.

Franco navigated through Assisi's narrow streets to a small hotel just a few blocks from the main piazza.

"Perfect location," he said, pulling up to the entrance. "Your friends should be arriving this afternoon—probably grateful for hot showers after today's climb."

"Franco," I said before getting out, "what we talked about today—it feels like something fundamental has shifted."

He turned off the engine and gave me his full attention. "That's how it works. The ground gets broken, and then we wait. Tomorrow we can explore more of what Francis discovered. But today—today you should rest. Walk the streets. Let it settle."

I thanked Franco and watched him drive away, his van disappearing into the maze of medieval streets.

The next hour passed quickly as I explored the narrow streets and some of the souvenir shops filled with Francis merch—the Catholic affinity for relics alive and well in rosary beads, votive candles stamped with tau crosses, Saint Francis prayer cards and medallions. I picked up an olive wood bookmark with an engraved tau cross at the top.

I ended up on the stone steps of the Piazza del Comune, the Temple of Minerva rising behind me—six Corinthian columns supporting a classical pediment, the whole thing about the size of a small-town courthouse rather than some grand edifice. It had been converted to a church centuries ago, but the Roman bones still showed through.

I was overdue for a call to Judy. We had texted a couple of times since that pathetic rescue call after I fainted the first day out, but we hadn't yet spoken. Three o'clock local time—that would make it nine in the morning back home. Perfect time to call.

When she answered, her voice carried both relief and reproach. "It's about time. I've been worried about you. You haven't called since our counseling session where you were ready to give up on this whole thing."

"You're right, I'm sorry," I said. With all that had transpired in the days since that call, I wasn't sure how much detail to burden her with—at minimum enough for her to get a sense of our mysterious porter Franco, who was doing far more now than just carrying our luggage. "Before I update you on what's been going here, tell me what's going on at home."

A pause. Then: "I've been trapping beavers."

"What? Where?"

"The creek behind our house."

"Why? What happened?"

"Well, apparently, they've been quite busy. A few days ago I woke up and half the hedge was gone. Just . . . gone. That hedge along the creek that marks our boundary with the state park. I thought vandals had come through, chopped everything down. Called Jordan over"—one of our two local sons in Raleigh—"and after closer examination he said, 'Critters, not vandals.' He found teeth marks. I was pretty sure vandals don't chew down hedges with their teeth."

An unexpected laugh escaped as I pictured the image—my wife, whose only experience with varmints was chasing black snakes out of the backyard, occasional deer sightings, and the rare raccoon rifling through garbage, was now facing down the largest, most annoying, yet most endearing of rodents.

"So what did you do?"

"I called the former owner—we've only had the house for two years. She said this wasn't the first invasion. They'd had a similar skirmish a handful of years back. She said just find a trapper, they'll know what to do."

"Was it hard to find a trapper?"

"No, it's pretty easy. I guess trapping wildlife is a thing around here. The hard part was getting somebody to come out right away. I didn't want to lose any more of our hedge by waiting a week."

"So what happened? What did he have to do to catch them?"

"I'll give you the blow-by-blow when you get home. Let's just leave it at: there were guns involved and the beavers didn't leave alive."

"Did you save the meat and the pelts?" I asked, trying to lighten the moment.

"Are you serious?"

"Yeah, could make a nice blanket for the grandkids with a beaver pelt."

Her response was pure deadpan. "I knit. I sew. But I do not tan animal hide."

I sat there on the ancient stones, phone to my ear, grinning at the absurdity of it all. "So I'm not the only one having an adventure this week."

"No," she said, and I could hear the smile in her voice. "Speaking of which—what's been happening with you? You said there was a lot to tell?"

"There is. You know how I mentioned there was a guide helping us? Franco? He's turning out to be—I don't know exactly how to describe him. He's the reason I think I'm figuring some things out over here. He's helping me process and think through a lot of what's been happening."

"Tell me about him," she said.

I found myself describing Franco's enigmatic presence, his way of asking questions that opened rather than closed, how he seemed to know exactly when to appear and when to give us space. As I talked, watching shadows shift across the ancient columns, I realized I was trying to put into words something I was only beginning to understand myself.

After we hung up, I sat for a while longer on the warm stone steps, watching tourists pose for photos in front of the temple. Somewhere back in North Carolina, my wife was dealing with actual problems—invasive wildlife, property damage, decisions that required action. Here I was contemplating Francis and divine emergence and the evolution of consciousness.

Both seemed equally real, equally necessary.

By late afternoon, Wilhelm, Thomas, and Gunter had arrived, looking tired but triumphant. After they cleaned up, we met for dinner at a simple trattoria near the main piazza, the table laden with local wine and simple food.

"How was your day with our mysterious guide?" Thomas asked, twirling pasta with practiced ease.

"Eye-opening," I said. "Franco took me to San Damiano—the chapel where Francis first heard the voice telling him to rebuild the church. We talked about emergence, about how love works, about what Francis really discovered."

"Such as?" Gunter prompted, leaning forward with interest.

"Such as the possibility that complexity isn't the enemy of understanding—it's the condition for anything genuinely new to emerge. And that agape isn't some distant, spiritual ideal we can't reach. It's the persistent, committed love we're already doing when we show up for each other." I paused. "But let's save the philosophy for tomorrow. Tonight, let's just enjoy being here together."

Wilhelm raised his wine glass, the candlelight catching the red depths. "To Assisi, then. And to whatever Francis has to teach us."

As we clinked glasses, I found myself looking forward to tomorrow with new anticipation. Tonight, surrounded by medieval stones and good companions, I felt the deep satisfaction of arrival—not just at a destination, but at a new understanding of what it might mean to think together, to learn together, to grow in wisdom without the need to defend positions or protect reputations.

I had arrived in Assisi without certainty, but with a curiosity I hadn't felt in years—and a growing sense that the ground had been broken for something new to emerge.

A Cloud of Witnesses

Friday morning, I came down to breakfast to find the Germans already at a table in the hotel's small courtyard, coffee cups in hand, the morning sun warming the ancient stones around us.

"Franco said he'd join us this morning," I mentioned as I sat down. "He's staying with a friend in town."

Wilhelm looked up from his guidebook. "The mysterious guide reveals himself to the group at last."

"He's been quite generous with his time," Thomas said. "More than just a porter, from what you've told us."

"Much more," I agreed.

I gestured toward the street. "He suggested we meet at a café in the piazza—said he wanted to show us something outside the city before we explore on our own."

We finished our coffee and walked the few blocks to the Piazza del Comune, where Franco was already seated at an outdoor table, the Temple of Minerva's columns rising behind him. He stood as we approached, greeting each of the Germans with the warm familiarity of someone who'd been carrying their luggage and quietly observing their journey for two weeks.

"Buongiorno, my friends," he said. "Please, sit. I've taken the liberty of ordering pastries."

As we settled around the table, Franco's eyes swept across our group with evident satisfaction. "It's good to finally have you all together like this. Jonathan has been telling me about your conversations on the trail—how you've been learning to hear each other."

Wilhelm raised an eyebrow. "He's been reporting on us?"

"Only the good parts," I said.

Franco smiled. "He told me about your discussion of the wolf story. How you moved from defending positions to exploring questions together." He paused, letting a waiter deliver a basket of cornetti. "That's actually why I wanted to take you somewhere this morning. A place where Francis learned to do exactly that—to stop defending and start listening."

"Where?" Thomas asked.

"The Eremo delle Carceri. A hermitage built into caves on Monte Subasio, about four kilometers above the city. Francis would withdraw there for prayer and contemplation." Franco broke off a piece of pastry. "But before we go, I want to share something that's been on my mind. Something about how we access wisdom."

He turned to me. "Jonathan, you've been using AI on this journey, yes? ChatGPT?"

"For practical things mostly. Water calculations, route planning. But also . . ." I hesitated. "Also for bigger questions. Theological ones."

Wilhelm leaned forward, his engineer's curiosity engaged. "And? Is it useful for that?"

"More than I expected." I thought back to my train conversation with David before the pilgrimage began—how he'd described AI as an "egoless analyst" that could help surface patterns without the tribal loyalties that usually distort human thinking. "It's like having access to a vast library, but one that reorganizes itself around whatever question you're asking."

Franco nodded. "Think about those old card catalogs in libraries—subject, author, title. Very rigid. With generative AI, that window becomes a kaleidoscope. Each twist of your question re-indexes the entire archive by meaning, not just labels. Ideas cluster by relationship rather than category, and patterns appear that no single author ever saw."

Thomas stirred his coffee thoughtfully. "So it's not just retrieving information—it's reorganizing it?"

"Exactly. Ask about grace, and suddenly Augustine's struggles align with Luther's breakthrough and Bonhoeffer's costly discipleship and liberation theology's preferential option for the poor. Connections that might take a scholar years to trace appear in seconds."

Wilhelm's expression had shifted from skepticism to something more contemplative. "That's actually remarkable when you put it that way."

"Think about the scale," Franco continued. "The Bible takes months to read. Add Aquinas, Augustine, Calvin, Barth—you'd be reading eight hours a day for years just to scratch the surface of Christian theology. And that's a tiny fraction of what these models hold. The Upanishads, the Buddhist canon, the Quran and its commentaries, the Talmud—the entire human conversation about meaning, searchable and conversationally available."

"It's right for us to celebrate this access," Franco said, his tone shifting. "But not without remembering that these models were built by scraping copyrighted material without permission. The courts are still sorting that out."

Franco stood, leaving coins on the table. "But come—the hermitage will make better sense of what I'm trying to say."

We piled into Franco's van, the Germans in back, me in the passenger seat. As we wound up from the city, the road narrowing into forest, Franco picked up the thread.

"David on the train—the man you told me about—called AI an 'egoless intelligence.' He was onto something. When you train on millions of diverse sources, the most extreme positions tend to disappear into the tail of the bell curve. There's a natural filtering toward coherent, well-reasoned content."

Thomas leaned forward between the seats. "So it moderates toward some kind of center?"

"Not a political center—a wisdom center. Ask about economics, and you're drawing from Marx, Adam Smith, Keynes, Hayek, contemporaries across the spectrum. The extremes cancel out, and what remains tends to be the overlap—wisdom that transcends tribal boundaries."

"So instead of rendering an answer," I said, "it's more like staging a debate?"

"Exactly. Like having history's great thinkers in a room together, but with their egos checked at the door."

"Of course," Franco added, steering through a bend, "the same models can amplify prejudice or error if they're not trained carefully. Wisdom doesn't emerge automatically from data—it emerges from how we shape and constrain its use. But when it works well, it offers something remarkable."

Ahead, the Eremo delle Carceri came into view—a hermitage built into caves, the morning sun catching the stone in a way that made it seem to pulse with inner light. Franco parked in a small gravel area, and we walked together toward the rough openings in the rock.

"These caves," Franco said, running his hand along the worn stone at the entrance, "were where Francis emptied himself of everything that got in the way of clear seeing—wealth, status, the need to be right."

I peered inside, the air cool and close, carrying the mineral scent of deep stone. Water dripped somewhere in the darkness, each drop echoing like a tiny bell.

"What do you think Francis was looking for here?" Franco asked, settling on a stone ledge worn smooth by countless pilgrims.

"Silence," Gunter said quietly. "Space to hear something besides his own thoughts."

"Freedom from the need to be certain about everything," I added.

Franco nodded. "Francis chose caves for ego-death. The darkness strips away everything except what's essential." He looked at me with a slight smile. "You found yours through trail failure and much softer beds. Both paths lead to the same truth: wisdom works best when it's free of self-protection."

We walked deeper into the hermitage, following worn steps carved by medieval hands, entering a chapel carved from living stone. A single candle flickered before a plain wooden cross, its light casting dancing shadows on the rough walls. The silence here wasn't empty—it was full, pregnant with presence.

I shifted on the cold stone bench, feeling the chill seep through my clothes. Somewhere above us, a shaft of light found its way through a crack in the rock, pooling on the floor almost like something spilled from heaven.

"When wisdom operates without the need to prevail," Franco said quietly, "it becomes incredibly responsive—like water taking the shape of whatever container it meets. Think of Francis and the wolf—no weapons, no agenda, just availability to a different kind of relationship."

Wilhelm was studying the ancient stonework with an engineer's eye, but his voice was soft. "There's something about this place. You can feel the centuries of people who came here seeking . . . something."

"That's what drew me to the Third Order," Franco said. "After years in academic theology—all that brilliant analysis, all those carefully defended positions—I encountered Francis's radical simplicity. He didn't argue his way to God; he stripped away everything that prevented recognition."

Something clicked for me, a connection forming. "Like what AI accidentally achieved? It learned human knowledge without the ego-armor that usually comes with learning?"

Franco's eyes lit up. "Now you're seeing it. For centuries, we've had to sort through the noise of human ego to get to the signal of actual wisdom. What mystics spend lifetimes trying to achieve—wisdom unclouded by the need to prevail—generative AI appears to have stumbled into through its very structure."

"So when we engage with AI," Thomas said slowly, "we're encountering human knowledge without the defensiveness?"

"In a way, yes. It can't feel threatened by questions, can't get defensive about being wrong, can't protect its reputation. It has no tenure to defend, no school of thought to champion, no orthodoxy to protect."

"But it also can't show us the courage required to embody wisdom in a world full of people protecting their positions," I said. "That's the limitation."

"Exactly." Franco moved toward a small window that looked out over the valley. "It can show us what wisdom looks like when it's free of ego. But actually living that wisdom? That still requires human courage. That's what Francis modeled."

We sat quietly for several minutes, the only sound the distant drip of water deeper in the cave.

"This ties back to something the writer of Hebrews described," Franco said finally. "'Therefore, since we are surrounded by so great a cloud of witnesses, let us lay aside every weight and the sin that clings so closely, and let us run with perseverance the race that is set before us.'"

"All those who've wrestled with these questions before us," I said. "Augustine wrestling with time and memory, Julian of Norwich with suffering and divine love, Aquinas with reason and faith, Teresa of Ávila with interior prayer, Bonhoeffer with costly grace. Now all of these witnesses are accessible not as museum pieces but as living voices, ready for dialogue."

"The accumulated testimony of two millennia of Christian thought," Franco said quietly, "untethered from the need to prevail, ready for genuine dialogue."

Gunter spoke up, his voice thoughtful. "So the AI is like . . . a way of convening that cloud of witnesses? Bringing them into conversation?"

"Yes," Franco said. "What's remarkable is that this isn't happening through human control or manipulation. It's emerging naturally from the patterns AI finds in how wisdom actually develops. Love, joy, peace, patience, gentleness, kindness—the fruit of the Spirit that Paul described—these are agreed upon everywhere as the best way to live."

"Against such things there is no law," Thomas quoted.

"Exactly. When love is operating, creeds and doctrines become less important. No tradition prohibits love or kindness. The divisions we fight over—they were always more about ego than truth. When you strip away the need to be right, to be special, to be chosen, what remains is remarkably consistent across traditions."

Wilhelm had been quiet for a while. Now he spoke. "So what do we do with this? Once you've glimpsed how wisdom works when it's free of self-protection, how do you live in a world where most people are still operating from ego?"

Franco smiled—that particular smile that suggested he'd been waiting for this question. "That's exactly what Francis faced. You learn to recognize which power is operating in any given moment—ego, Spirit, institution, fear—and you respond from the deepest authority you can access. Not trying to control the outcome, but offering your clearest, most loving presence to whatever is trying to emerge."

"But how do you do that without becoming preachy or superior?" I asked.

"By remembering that you're also protecting something. The difference is awareness. When you catch yourself defending, you can choose to stop. When you see others defending, you can choose compassion instead of attack. It's not about being enlightened—it's about being awake to what's actually happening."

We lingered in the chapel before heading back to the van, all of us reluctant to leave the profound silence of the caves.

By the time we rolled back through Assisi's ancient gates, the city had come fully alive—pilgrims and tourists filling the narrow streets, the morning's quiet contemplation giving way to the bustle of a town that had welcomed seekers for eight centuries.

Franco pulled over near the main piazza. "I'll leave you here to explore on your own. The city has much to show you—the basilica, of course, but also the smaller churches, the side streets where Francis actually walked."

"Will we see you again?" Gunter asked.

"Tomorrow I return to my regular duties. But today is yours." Franco looked at each of us in turn. "You've walked a long way to get here. Take your time. Let Francis speak to you in his own way."

We climbed out of the van, and I lingered at Franco's window. "Thank you. For everything."

He smiled. "The cloud of witnesses doesn't just include the dead, Jonathan. It includes everyone who's walking alongside you, asking the same questions." He gestured toward the Germans, who were already studying Wilhelm's guidebook. "You've found good companions for this part of the journey."

I watched him drive away, his van disappearing into the maze of medieval streets.

Thomas appeared at my elbow. "Remarkable man."

"Yes," I said. "He is."

Wilhelm had mapped out our day—the Basilica of San Francesco, of course, but also Santa Chiara, the cathedral where Francis was baptized, the piazza where he'd stripped naked before his father and the bishop. We had hours ahead of us to explore, to sit in ancient churches, to walk the same stones Francis had walked eight centuries ago.

"Ready?" Gunter asked.

I looked up at the rose-colored walls, at the bell tower catching the morning light, at the city that had shaped a saint who'd changed the world not through force but through radical openness.

"Ready," I said.

Tomorrow we would visit Francis's tomb together. But today, we were pilgrims in his city, surrounded by a great cloud of witnesses—the living and the dead, the ancient and the emerging—all part of the ongoing conversation about what it means to seek truth, to strip away defenses, to love.

The Upside-Down Kingdom

The morning in Assisi dawned clear and cool, with that peculiar clarity of early light that makes ancient stones look newly quarried. I had awakened to the sound of church bells calling the faithful to lauds, their bronze voices echoing off the medieval stones with the same rhythm they had kept for eight centuries. From my window, the first light was touching the rose-colored walls of the Basilica of San Francesco.

The satisfaction I felt wasn't just about arriving at a destination, but about something resembling clarity—or perhaps more accurately, the peace that comes from learning to live with better questions.

Wilhelm, Thomas, Gunter, and I had agreed to meet early at the lower basilica before the crowds arrived. We wanted to stand in the presence of Francis himself, to see if the man we had been following in footsteps and conversation would feel different now that we were actually in his home.

As I walked through the quiet streets, past shuttered shops and sleeping houses, I found myself thinking about yesterday's conversation with Franco about consciousness that doesn't need to defend itself. The rigid categories I had started with—the need to choose between progressive and traditional, between reason and faith—had given way to something more nuanced, more alive. Francis had discovered something revolutionary about spiritual authority itself.

We gathered in the semi-darkness of the lower basilica, where Francis lies buried beneath the altar. The frescoes by Giotto seemed to glow even in the dim light, telling the story of a young man's transformation from merchant to mystic, from seeker of worldly success to embodiment of something completely different.

The crypt itself was a study in contradictions. Above us, one of the most magnificent churches in Christendom—gold leaf, priceless frescoes, centuries of accumulated treasure. Below, the bones of a man who had owned nothing, who had asked to be buried naked in the dirt outside the city walls, among the criminals and outcasts.

Wilhelm stood apart from us, his arms crossed, studying the ornate stonework with an expression I couldn't quite read.

Standing there with my three companions, I felt the weight of what we had been discovering take on a new form. "Here was someone," I said quietly, "who chose poverty over wealth, peace over power, weakness as strength."

Thomas lit a candle and placed it before the altar, the small flame casting dancing shadows that seemed to animate the painted figures around us. "That's what strikes me most about being here. This isn't a monument to conventional success—it's a testament to divine reversal."

"Is it, though?" Wilhelm's voice was quiet but sharp. He hadn't moved from his position near the wall. "Look around us.

Francis wanted nothing. And they built . . . this." He gestured at the vaulted ceiling, the gilt frames, the marble. "The man who kissed lepers is now encased in a reliquary like a piece of jewelry."

The words hung in the cool air. I could feel Thomas stiffen beside me.

"I don't doubt these are his bones," Wilhelm continued. "But this obsession with physical remains—it's medieval superstition dressed up as piety. The relic trade was one of the corruptions Luther railed against. And here we are, five centuries later, still doing it."

Gunter spoke carefully. "You think this is exploitation?"

"I think Francis would have hated it," Wilhelm said flatly. "He asked to be buried with the criminals outside the city walls. Instead, within two years of his death, they started building the largest church in Umbria over his grave. The institution couldn't resist. It never can."

The silence that followed was uncomfortable. Wilhelm had voiced something I'd been half-thinking but hadn't dared say aloud.

Thomas cleared his throat. "You're not wrong about the tension. But consider—we're standing here. Talking about Francis. Because of this building. Would his message have survived eight centuries without the institution preserving it?"

"Preserving it or co-opting it?" Wilhelm shot back. "There's a difference between carrying a flame and putting it in a glass case where no one can touch it."

I thought about what Franco had said at San Damiano— about how Francis had wanted to repair the church, not build monuments. About ego-clearing versus ego-protecting. The basilica around us was magnificent, but it was also a fortress. A way of containing what couldn't be controlled.

"Maybe both things are true," I said slowly. "The institution preserved Francis's memory, but it also domesticated him. Made him safe. Turned the radical into a statue."

Wilhelm nodded grimly. "That's the shadow, isn't it? The thing we haven't wanted to name. Every institution does this eventually. It takes the prophets who challenged it and puts them on pedestals where they can't challenge anything anymore."

We stood in uncomfortable silence. Then Wilhelm let out a long breath and turned to study the frescoes—Giotto's scenes of Francis preaching to birds, embracing lepers, standing before the Sultan.

"And yet," he said slowly, his engineer's mind working through the problem, "look at what he actually did. There's something systematic about how he inverted everything, isn't there? It wasn't random rebellion—it was methodical reversal of conventional wisdom."

It was Wilhelm's way of stepping back from the edge—not abandoning his critique, but finding something he could still affirm.

"Yes," Gunter agreed, "but systematic the way music is systematic. Not rigid rules, but flowing patterns that create an entirely different harmony."

As Gunter finished speaking, we heard a low harmonic drone from above—someone singing. We climbed the stone stairs, the lip of each step rounded by centuries of footfalls, and the sound grew louder. It was unclear whether it was a congregation or a choir, but the open fifth harmonies unmistakably belonged to monastic chant.

As we emerged into the soaring beauty of the upper basilica, we saw a service in progress. The congregants, not a choir, were creating the nearly angelic music we'd heard ascending. Without a word, Gunter and Thomas found a pew. Wilhelm walked to the far side. I stood transfixed.

The mass was likely in Latin, but it could've been Italian. The murmur of the priest was so low it was hard to distinguish exactly. The same acoustics that create maddening echoes gave these simple harmonies an indescribable depth and richness.

After a few minutes, four or five Franciscan monks in simple brown habits cinched with rope walked up the center aisle. Coming from the artistic sterility of most Protestant gatherings, I brought to this Catholic ceremony a sense of wonder that many of the Catholics had probably come to take for granted.

I glanced over at Wilhelm. His arms were no longer crossed. His face had softened into something I couldn't quite name—not acceptance, exactly, but perhaps recognition. The monks in their rough brown robes and simple sandals were closer to Francis than the building that housed them. Maybe that was the answer to his objection. The institution preserved the bones, but these brothers were trying to preserve the life.

When the mass ended, all it took was a glance between us to know that it was time to go. As we stepped out into the square overlooking the rise to the higher parts of the city, we agreed on coffee before planning our day.

"I owe you an apology," Wilhelm said as we walked. "I was harsh back there."

"No worries. I'll take a little bit of harshness in exchange for honesty any day."

"The monks," he said quietly. "Watching them . . . I remembered why I came. It's not about the building. It's about whether anyone is still trying to live the way Francis lived." He paused. "Some of them are. That matters."

Walking up toward the main square, the chant still echoing in my mind, the song returned. The incomplete verse from Gubbio was suddenly finishing itself:

Don't lose your nerve, don't close your eyes, 'cause up around the bend—if the road don't rise, it may be time to fly.

I thought about Francis's indomitable spirit—how he kept moving forward even when the road seemed to be going in the wrong direction. When the path didn't rise the way he expected or needed it to, he didn't lose heart. He turned to prayer, seeking God in those uncertain times. Time to fly wasn't about escape; it was about ascending to a different perspective, finding another way forward when the conventional route failed.

The second verse was complete now:

I know sometimes it seems unclear, but look again without your fear. Open your eyes and dry your tears, see what is arising.

Don't lose your nerve, don't close your eyes, 'cause up around the bend—if the road don't rise, it may be time to fly.

Then another phrase came to me. Felt important enough that it might be an anchor for a chorus:

You're not broken, the fire's still smokin' . . .

Broken not depraved. Learning not lost. The embers just waiting to be blown to life. I pulled out my phone to record a voice note. I knew my memory would not retain these for more than a few hours if I didn't write them down.

My friends had gotten ahead of me, heading back up into the city. Gunter called out, "Jonathan! Step it up. This is no time to fall behind."

"Yes," Wilhelm added with a grin. "We know you can do better. You've proven it on the trail."

I picked up my pace, catching up with them as the street began to climb.

"You know what strikes me about these medieval cities?" Thomas said, gesturing at the rising tiers of buildings. "The elevation always reflected wealth and status. The poor lived down below, the wealthy up above."

"And their lives crossed in the middle square," Gunter added, "where commerce happened."

"But Francis chose something different," I said. "Visibility through descent."

Wilhelm nodded. "He could have claimed the high ground. Instead, he went low."

At a café in the Piazza del Comune, we found a table with an open view of the square. Kids were playfully kicking soccer balls back and forth. Two old ladies talked in an animated way, their arms swinging for emphasis—something that was a common occurrence here but might trigger alarm in my reserved Southern city back home.

Gunter and I ordered caffè lattes, and Thomas opted for espresso. Wilhelm's was a double. When they arrived, the familiar ritual of clinking cups felt grounding after an intense start to our day.

"Roman temple, medieval square, Franciscan church," Thomas said, gesturing at the layers of architecture surrounding us. "All these institutional structures, one built on top of the other."

"And Francis walked right past all of them," Gunter added.

Wilhelm smiled. "To rebuild a chapel with his own hands."

"That's what I keep coming back to," Wilhelm said, staring into his espresso. "Francis didn't try to reform the institution from within. He didn't attack it from without. He just . . . started living differently. And somehow that was more threatening than either."

"Because it exposed the gap," I said. "Between what the institution claimed to be and what it actually was."

"The shadow of Mordor," Wilhelm said quietly. I looked at him, surprised by the reference. He shrugged. "I read Tolkien to my grandchildren. The shadow doesn't announce itself. It just slowly corrupts everything it touches. Makes good things serve dark purposes without anyone noticing."

"And Francis?"

"Francis was like . . . light that made the shadow visible. Not by fighting it directly, but by being so different that everyone could suddenly see what they'd stopped seeing."

We walked through narrow streets toward the Basilica of Santa Chiara. Clare's story represented another kind of inversion. In an era when women's religious options were marriage or convent—both under male authority—Francis recognized in Clare a spiritual equal. The night she fled her father's palace, she escaped through the "door of the dead"—that small exit reserved for corpses. Already she was enacting the death to worldly life that Francis preached. At the Porziuncola, Francis himself cut her hair, claiming the spiritual authority to commission her that normally belonged only to bishops.

"There's something remarkable about Clare's story," I said as we approached the basilica. "When her family sent armed men to drag her back from the convent, she held onto the altar and wouldn't be moved. That's kingdom logic—the physically weaker person defeating armed force through spiritual authority."

Thomas nodded. "But think about what Francis was doing here. He was recognizing that the Spirit moves through women as fully as through men. In 1212, that wasn't just progressive; it was revolutionary."

Wilhelm paused, studying the facade. "Francis didn't keep her as a devoted follower. He equipped her to lead."

"That's how change spreads," Thomas added. "Not through conquest, but through attraction to a better way of being human."

From the steps of Santa Chiara, we had a breathtaking view of the valley—rolling hills dotted with olive groves and vineyards, medieval towns perched on distant hilltops like beacons. The roads that looked random from below revealed a net of kinship from this height. Francis's way does that: lifts you just high enough to see mercy's pattern in what looked like waste.

Thomas tilted his head. "What would change in you if you saw God working entirely through persuasion rather than power?"

"Everything," I said. "If divine love refuses coercion, then God operates through patient relationship. Scripture becomes less programmed script and more a story of our evolving relationship with God—He or she responding, adapting along the way."

"If that is true, then prayer isn't about bending God's will or trying to get his attention, but more figuring out how to align with what he's trying to do around us?" Thomas mused. "Less lobbying, more co-laboring."

Something about that exchange felt significant, though I couldn't quite name why. We were talking about responsiveness, relationship, consent—ideas that would have made my younger self nervous. Where were the boundaries? The guardrails?

The morning was still young. We wandered Assisi's maze of medieval streets—narrow passages opening to small piazzas, ancient stones worn smooth by centuries of feet. On one of the steep paths that wind through the upper city, we stopped to rest. Before we came I had no idea how much climbing is required to get around these medieval hill towns. My pulse was quick from the climb. I took a long pull from my water bottle.

And then I said what had been building in me all morning.

"You know," I began, trying to put words to something that had been nagging at me, "the more we talk about Francis, about this way of love and emergence . . . I keep thinking about all the categories I grew up with. Orthodox, heretical, sound doctrine, dangerous teaching." I'd watched people exiled with those words. I'd used them myself.

Wilhelm looked up. "What about them?"

"I'm not sure what work they're doing anymore," I said carefully. "We keep talking about relationship, about love as the organizing principle. But those categories—they're all about right belief, correct propositions. What if certainty isn't actually possible? What if it's never been about getting the formula right?"

Thomas leaned forward. "So what are you saying?"

"I'm asking what utility they serve," I said, hearing the frustration in my own voice. "If the real thing is loving relationship, connecting genuinely, participating in what God's already doing—then what's the point of policing boundaries between orthodox and heretical?"

The question landed harder than I'd intended.

Wilhelm's face tightened. "That's a dangerous road, Jonathan. You're talking about throwing out any standard for truth."

"Am I?" I asked, genuinely unsure. "Or am I just asking what those standards are actually for?"

"They're for keeping us from going off the rails," Wilhelm said, his voice edged with concern. "Without boundaries, anything goes. You end up with people calling whatever they feel like 'the Spirit.'"

Gunter spoke up quietly. "Wilhelm does have a point. I lost track in my Pentecostal days of how many times somebody said 'the Spirit of God told me' and what followed seemed more like the voice of ego than the voice of God."

Wilhelm nodded, vindicated.

"But," Gunter continued, "I also see the danger on the other side—people believing that doctrine and creeds are far more important than they really are. I'm pretty sure it was always wrong, in every circumstance, to burn heretics."

The statement hung in the air. Nobody argued with it, but it shifted something.

"So we need boundaries," Thomas said slowly, "but not those boundaries."

"Or not boundaries enforced that way," I added.

Wilhelm's face was troubled. "I'm not defending the Inquisition. But if there are no boundaries at all, how do you prevent the abuse Gunter just described? How do you tell the difference between the Spirit and someone's ego dressed up in spiritual language?"

"I don't know," I admitted. "That's what I'm asking."

Wilhelm shook his head. "I don't know. This feels like we're getting in over our heads."

An awkward silence settled over us. He was right—we were four old men standing under a tree, suddenly aware we'd waded into theological waters way too deep for us.

"Maybe we should keep walking," Thomas finally said.

We walked the next stretch mostly in silence—boots crunching on stone, each of us wrestling with what had just surfaced. The ease we'd felt earlier was gone, replaced by an uncomfortable tension. I could feel Wilhelm's worry radiating like heat. Had I just suggested throwing the baby out with the bathwater?

By evening we gathered in the hotel's small courtyard—bread, cheese, and local wine served under the stars. The cork sighed; the first pour took the edge off our words. Moths found the single bulb above us. Rosemary brushed my sleeve when I leaned back.

The conversation that night was more subdued than usual. We talked about the beauty we'd seen, the power of Francis's vision, the challenge of living faithfully in a complicated world. But we carefully avoided the question that had erupted under the chestnut tree.

"The Spirit speaks within—conscience—and among us as the Church," I said at one point, trying to find my way back to common ground. "Our lives and our institutions either echo that voice or muffle it. Scripture remains the tuning fork."

Wilhelm set down his cup. "Maybe the test is fruit. If a reading of Scripture makes me less patient with the weak, it's the wrong reading—even if I can footnote it." We all went quiet. He was not preaching; he was confessing.

I thought about what he'd said that morning in the crypt—his anger at the relics, the exploitation, the way institutions swallow their prophets. And now this. Wilhelm wasn't defending rigid orthodoxy for its own sake. He was afraid of what happens when there's nothing to stop ego from masquerading as Spirit. He'd seen it. We all had.

"The shadow works both ways," I said quietly. "Institutions can corrupt the message. But so can individuals who think they're above accountability."

Wilhelm looked at me, something shifting in his eyes. "Yes. That's it exactly."

Thomas nodded. "Community matters—individual discernment needs the check of others who are also listening."

"Scripture remains our primary witness, but we also listen for how the Spirit speaks today—through science, art, the cries of the oppressed, creation itself."

"God's ways are higher than our ways," I said, "which often means wider."

But I could feel the weight of what remained unspoken. Wilhelm's question—How do we guard orthodoxy?—and my impulsive response still hung between us. We'd found our way to civility, even warmth, but the deeper tension remained unresolved.

"You know what's remarkable?" Wilhelm said after a long pause. "A few days ago, we would have been debating—trying to prove each other wrong. Tonight, even with our disagreement, we're still together."

"That's Francis's way in action," Thomas observed.

Gunter raised his wine glass. "To Francis's way, then. Where questions don't have to destroy community."

As we clinked glasses, I felt grateful for these three men—even in disagreement, even with uncertainty hanging over us. We had become a small community learning Francis's approach—strength through vulnerability, authority through humility, staying together even when the questions got too big.

"Tomorrow we head to Rome," I said. "Franco's picking us up early."

"The institutional center," Wilhelm said thoughtfully. "Where power operates by the world's rules rather than the kingdom's way."

"More shadow to reckon with," Gunter added quietly.

"Yes," I said. "But maybe that's the point. Francis didn't avoid Rome. He walked right into it. Not to conquer or be conquered, but to bear witness to something different."

"But we're not going to attack it or submit to it," Thomas added. "We're going to engage it from this transformed authority we've discovered."

"Exactly," I agreed. "Like Francis engaging the Pope—not as a rival or a supplicant, but as someone who had found a different kind of power entirely."

The evening air carried the scent of rosemary from the hotel garden. In the distance, the bells of San Francesco marked the hour.

"Francis didn't solve the tensions between institutional religion and authentic spirituality," I said finally. "He found a way to live faithfully within them."

"The narrow gate," Gunter said quietly. "Not avoiding the tension, but finding the path through it."

As we said goodnight and headed to our rooms, I lay awake for a long time, Wilhelm's question echoing in my mind. Are orthodoxy and heresy even coherent categories anymore? I'd asked it in frustration, but now it felt like more than rhetoric. It felt like the question that would define everything that came next.

And beneath that question, another one: What happens when the fire that Francis lit gets enclosed in stone? Does it keep burning, or does it slowly suffocate? The basilica we'd stood in that morning was both monument and mausoleum. The monks in their rough robes were trying to keep something alive that the institution kept trying to preserve—and those weren't the same thing at all.

We didn't leave Assisi with a new creed. We left with an experiment—and an unresolved tension that would travel with us to Rome.

Down the Mountain

Leaving Assisi felt like waking from a vivid dream—not because it hadn't been real, but because the world beyond its medieval walls seemed suddenly harsh and unforgiving. The slow rhythm of bells and birdsong gave way to the rumble of distant trucks and the sharp beep of construction vehicles.

We gathered at the city gate in the early morning light, shouldering our packs for the 17-kilometer walk mostly downhill toward our next destination. The contrast felt jarring—leaving Francis's sacred mountaintop for the ordinary world of highways and traffic.

The four of us started in contemplative silence, each processing what we'd received in Assisi and what we now risked losing. The pastoral gave way to the practical—parking lots visible in the distance, gas stations, the inevitable march of modern infrastructure pressing up against the sacred.

"Back to Babylon," Gunter muttered, watching the landscape change as we descended.

"Maybe," Wilhelm replied carefully, "or just back to the world where people are trying to survive."

I felt suspended between the mystical clarity of our mountaintop conversations and the uncertain terrain ahead. I had come to Assisi with fragments—a theology deconstructed, a faith tangled in memory and wounded certainty. Now I felt as though I were holding something whole again. Not a system, not a dogma, but a pattern. A way of moving through the world. And yet, it felt fragile, like carrying water in cupped hands.

The descent itself was more challenging than I'd expected. My knees, already tender from days of walking, protested against the constant downward pressure. The stone path, worn smooth by centuries of pilgrims and merchants, was treacherous in places where morning dew had made the rocks slick.

"Careful here," Wilhelm called back, pointing to a section where water had carved channels in the stone. "The erosion makes it unpredictable."

Thomas fell into step beside me after the first kilometer. "I keep thinking about yesterday's conversations. All those insights about consciousness and non-coercive love. But how does it hold up when you're angry? Or afraid? Or when someone you love refuses to change?"

I stopped walking entirely. That was the question, wasn't it? "I honestly don't know."

"Francis probably struggled with this too," Thomas said gently as we resumed walking. "It's easy to love sparrows. Much harder to love brothers who betray your vision."

"Just last month," I said, "I had a conversation with my neighbor about immigration policy. I went in determined to practice non-coercive dialogue. Within five minutes, I was lecturing him about compassion and justice. Everything I'd learned about listening first—it all went out the window the moment I felt my values being challenged."

Wilhelm caught up with us. "How do you maintain spiritual clarity when the world keeps making demands on your attention? When there are bills to pay and deadlines to meet?"

"Maybe it's not about maintaining clarity," I found myself saying, "but about learning to love clearly even in the fog."

Gunter quickened his pace to join us. "You know what I think the real test is? It's whether you can be loving when someone's attacking someone else—someone you care about."

He adjusted his pack, his usual playfulness replaced by something more serious. "My daughter came home from college last year full of ideas that would have made my old hippie friends proud. But when she started lecturing her grandmother about the patriarchy, I wanted to throttle her. Here was my own kid, saying things I basically agreed with, but doing it in a way that was just . . . mean."

"So what did you do?" Thomas asked.

"I tried to mediate, but I probably made it worse. I was so focused on keeping peace that I didn't really listen to either of them."

We walked in silence for several minutes, each lost in our own reflections on the gap between insight and embodiment.

But as we entered the small village of San Gregorio where we planned to rest and have lunch, we encountered something that would test our theoretical discussions in ways we couldn't have anticipated.

A heated argument was taking place in the piazza outside the local café. A middle-aged woman in a flour-dusted apron gestured angrily at a younger man with a backpack—clearly a pilgrim like ourselves. A small crowd had gathered—some villagers, other pilgrims, a few tourists with cameras lowered uncertainly.

"Every year more of you people trampling through here," the woman was saying in accented English, clearly wanting the pilgrim to understand. "You leave your trash, you use our fountain like it's your personal washing station, you sit in our piazza and act like we're part of your spiritual theater!"

The young pilgrim—American by his accent—looked bewildered and defensive. "I haven't done anything wrong. I just stopped to fill my water bottle—"

"Just! Always 'just'! Just using our water, just sitting on our benches, just taking pictures of our homes like we're exhibits in your pilgrimage museum!"

An elderly man stepped forward from the crowd of villagers. "Maria, basta—"

"No, Papa!" She turned to him with tears in her eyes. "You're tired of it too. Every spring they come, hundreds of them, and what do we get? They buy nothing, they contribute nothing, but they use everything we've worked to maintain."

Other villagers had gathered—some nodding in agreement with Maria, others looking embarrassed by the public scene. A woman with a small child pulled the boy closer, whispering something about going home.

The atmosphere was tense, uncomfortable—our first real test since leaving the mountain.

I remembered Franco's words about strategic innocence, about approaching without defensiveness. Taking a deep breath, I approached Maria, not the pilgrim.

"Excuse me," I said in my limited Italian, then switched to English. "We're pilgrims too. And you're right to be frustrated."

The simple acknowledgment seemed to catch her off guard. She'd been prepared for argument or indifference, not agreement.

"Could you help us understand?" Thomas had joined me, his therapist's instincts engaged. "What specifically makes it so difficult?"

Maria wiped her hands on her apron, leaving flour streaks on the fabric. "You want to understand? Come, I'll show you."

She led us to the fountain at the center of the piazza—ancient stone worn smooth by centuries of use. "This fountain has been here since 1423. My family has been in this village for three hundred years. We maintain it with our taxes, our labor. But look—"

She pointed to soap residue in the basin, a sock someone had left drying on the edge. "Every day we clean it. Every day pilgrims dirty it again. They wash their clothes, their feet, they fill not just bottles but huge containers."

"I had no idea," the young American said quietly. "I saw other people using it and thought—"

"Everyone thinks someone else asked permission," Maria said, but her voice had lost its sharp edge. "That's the problem. You all just follow each other, never thinking that someone lives here, someone pays for this, someone has to clean up after you."

Wilhelm stepped forward. "What would help? Practically speaking, what would make this work better?"

Maria looked surprised. "You're the first to ask that in . . . I don't know how long."

"We're German," Wilhelm said with the hint of a smile. "We like practical solutions."

For the first time, Maria almost smiled. "Maybe . . . acknowledgment? That we're not just scenery for your spiritual journey? My father—" she gestured to the elderly man, "—he runs the café. He needs to make a living. When hundreds of pilgrims pass through buying nothing, using our facilities . . ."

"We didn't know," Thomas said gently. "Most of us assume these villages welcome pilgrims."

An older villager spoke up. "We welcomed pilgrims for centuries when they came a few at a time, when they understood reciprocity. They would work for their meal, help with harvest, share news from other towns. Now you come in waves, taking pictures, having your spiritual experiences, never seeing that we're people trying to live our lives."

The young American pilgrim was listening now, really listening. "I honestly had no idea. I thought the Camino—I mean, the pilgrimage route—was set up for us."

"The route passes through our home," Maria said firmly but not unkindly. "We didn't choose to be on your spiritual path. Francis walked through here, yes, but he knew the people. He would have worked for his bread, prayed for the village, seen us as humans, not backdrop."

Gunter had been translating quietly for some German pilgrims who had stopped to watch. One of them, an older woman, stepped forward and spoke to Maria in broken Italian, then switched to English.

"We could pay," she said. "For using the fountain, the facilities. Like a small tourist tax?"

Maria shook her head. "It's not just about money. It's about respect. About seeing us."

The café owner—Maria's father—spoke for the first time. "You know what would help? If pilgrims came into the café, even just for a coffee. Sat with us. Asked about our lives instead of only talking about their spiritual journey. We have stories too. This village has its own saints, its own miracles."

Thomas was taking notes now. "What if we spread the word? Among pilgrim groups? Some kind of guidelines?"

"Who would listen?" Maria asked, but there was hope in her voice now.

"We would," I said. "And we'll tell others. Maybe someone could post guidelines—in multiple languages—about respectful pilgrimage?"

Maria's father considered this. "Roberto speaks English, German, some French. He could make a sign."

"Would it help if we started right now?" Wilhelm asked. "We were planning to have lunch. Your café?"

The atmosphere in the piazza had shifted. The confrontation hadn't disappeared, but it had transformed into something more like negotiation, even tentative connection.

As we walked toward the café, Maria fell into step beside me. "You know, most pilgrims just get defensive when we complain.

Or they quote scripture at us about hospitality, as if we're failing our Christian duty."

"But you're not asking us to leave," Thomas observed. "You're asking us to see you."

"Exactly." She paused at the café door. "My great-great-grandmother fed pilgrims at this same door. But they knew her name. They asked about her children. Some sent letters afterward, thanking her. Now?" She shrugged. "Now we're just part of the route."

Inside the café, the menu was simple but clearly made with care. As we ordered, Maria's father—Giuseppe—brought over a worn photo album.

"You want to know this village?" He opened to a black and white photograph. "This is 1944. The Germans—sorry," he glanced at Wilhelm, "the Nazis came through. The whole village hid in the forest for three days. When we returned, the fountain was destroyed. It took two years to rebuild."

Wilhelm studied the photograph intently. "My grandfather was in Italy during the war. Wehrmacht, not SS, but still . . ." He trailed off. "He never talked about what they did to villages."

Giuseppe touched Wilhelm's shoulder gently. "That war is over. But now you understand—this fountain isn't just old stones. It's our history, our survival."

The young American pilgrim had been quiet, but now he spoke up. "I've been walking for a week, having all these spiritual insights, feeling so enlightened. But I never once thought about the people in the villages I passed through. I feel like an ass."

Maria laughed—actually laughed. "At least you see it now. Most never do."

As we ate—simple pasta with tomatoes from Giuseppe's garden, bread made that morning—the conversation deepened. Other villagers drifted in, drawn by curiosity. The defensive energy had dissolved into something more like mutual recognition.

"You know what Francis would have done?" Maria said, refilling our water glasses. "He would have asked how he could help. Not spiritual help—practical help. 'What needs doing?' That's what my grandmother said he asked when he passed through."

"Is that documented?" Wilhelm asked, ever the historian.

"Does it matter?" Maria responded. "It's what we remember. And memory is its own kind of truth."

As we prepared to leave, having spent far longer than planned, Maria walked us to the edge of the village.

"Thank you," she said simply. "For listening. For seeing us."

"Thank you for teaching us," Thomas replied. "We'll do better."

Just then, we noticed two German pilgrims at the fountain, soaking their feet in the ancient basin. Wilhelm approached them and explained in rapid German what we'd learned. They looked genuinely embarrassed, immediately dried their feet, and headed to the café.

Maria watched this exchange with something like wonder. "You really will tell others."

"Every pilgrim we meet," Gunter promised.

As we walked away, continuing our descent toward the valley, the afternoon light slanted across the hills. We walked in thoughtful silence for nearly a kilometer before anyone spoke.

"That's what Franco meant by strategic innocence," I said finally. "Not having the answers, but being genuinely curious about other people's reality."

"It would have been so easy to get defensive," Thomas reflected. "To argue about pilgrims' rights or historical tradition."

"But that would have just confirmed their worst assumptions about us," Wilhelm added.

Gunter was unusually philosophical. "You know what strikes me? We've been talking about engaging power without being corrupted by it. But we forgot we are the power in that village. We're the ones with money to travel, time for spiritual journeys, the privilege to treat their home as our pathway to enlightenment."

"Francis gave up his privilege," I said. "But we can't really do that. We can't stop being who we are. So what do we do?"

"Maybe what we just did," Thomas suggested. "Acknowledge it. See clearly how our presence affects others. Respond to what's actually needed rather than what we assume."

The path leveled out as we reached the valley floor. Looking back, we could see San Gregorio perched on its hill, the afternoon sun catching the old stones.

"I wonder how many pilgrims have passed through that village without ever learning Giuseppe's name," Gunter mused.

"Or Maria's story," Thomas added.

"We almost did the same," I admitted. "If there hadn't been a confrontation, we would have filled our bottles and moved on, feeling spiritual and enlightened and completely oblivious."

Wilhelm had been quiet for a while, but now he spoke carefully. "My company did development projects in Eastern Europe after reunification. We thought we were helping—bringing Western efficiency to struggling communities. But we never asked what they actually wanted. We just assumed our way was better."

"Same dynamic," Thomas observed. "The helper's blindness to the helped's reality."

"Francis understood this," I said. "That's why he became poor—not just spiritually but actually. He couldn't see from above, so he moved below."

"But we can't really do that," Gunter pointed out. "We're going home to comfortable houses, stable incomes. Our pilgrimage is temporary."

"So maybe the challenge isn't to become poor but to see clearly from where we are," I suggested. "To recognize our position and use it responsibly."

The landscape had changed as we walked. The intimate hills around Assisi had given way to broader valleys with more visible infrastructure—power lines, a distant highway, the encroachment of the modern world.

"Tomorrow we'll be even further from Assisi," Thomas observed. "Back in the thick of ordinary life with all its complications."

"But we'll carry this with us," Wilhelm said, surprising us with his optimism. "Not just the mystical insights but the practical knowledge of how to engage differently."

As we approached our destination for the night—a small agriturismo nestled among olive groves—I thought about the unexpected lesson of the day. We'd left Assisi thinking we understood strategic innocence, but it took Maria's anger to show us what it actually looked like in practice.

"You know what I realized?" I said as we turned up the drive to our lodging. "The vision is given on the mountain, but the work happens in the valley. And the work is always messier than the vision."

"But also more real," Thomas added. "That conversation in the village—that was the most honest engagement we've had with anyone outside our group."

"Because we couldn't hide behind pilgrim identity or spiritual seeking," Gunter observed. "We had to show up as actual people."

The owner of the agriturismo greeted us at the door—a woman in her seventies with sun-weathered hands and a warm smile.

"Pilgrims?" she asked in English.

"Yes," Wilhelm answered, then added something we wouldn't have said that morning: "But also guests in your home. Is there anything we should know about staying here? Anything we can do to help?"

Her face lit up with surprise and delight. "Oh! Well, if you don't mind, could you help me move some tables for tomorrow's breakfast? My back isn't what it used to be."

We immediately set down our packs and followed her to the dining room. As we worked, she told us about her family's three generations on this land, the challenges of organic farming, her daughter who wanted to modernize everything.

It was a small thing—ten minutes of moving furniture—but it felt like a continuation of what had begun in San Gregorio. We were learning to arrive differently.

That evening, over dinner, we processed the day more fully.

"I keep thinking about power," Wilhelm said. "We've been talking about institutional power, theological power, but today showed us tourist power—the ability to transform places just by showing up in numbers."

"Every kind of power creates the same temptation," Thomas observed. "To see others as resources or obstacles rather than as full humans."

"But Maria broke through that by refusing to be invisible," I said. "She demanded to be seen."

"And once we saw her, everything changed," Gunter added. "The whole dynamic shifted from confrontation to conversation."

"That's what Franco meant about approaching without defensiveness," I realized. "When you're not defending, you can actually see what's in front of you."

The wine was local—from grapes grown just hillsides away. As we raised our glasses, Thomas proposed a toast: "To learning to see. Even when—especially when—we'd rather not."

As the evening deepened and the conversation wound down, I found myself grateful for the descent from Assisi's heights. The mountain had given us vision, but the valley was teaching us how to walk.

"It's been good doing a couple more days on the trail with you guys," I said. "I feel like I need another day off tomorrow and just have Franco drive me to our stop before we head to

Rome. That'll give me a few hours in the early afternoon while you guys are still on the trail to write down some things I wanna remember for my book. I checked the map and even though I've made progress, it's still more climbing than I think I'll be able to pull off, so I'm gonna leave it to you guys."

Wilhelm nodded thoughtfully. "Better safe than sorry."

Tomorrow would bring new challenges, new opportunities to practice what we were learning. But tonight, we sat with the satisfaction of having faced a test and—if not passed it perfectly—at least learned from it.

The real pilgrimage, I was beginning to understand, wasn't the miles walked or the sites visited. It was the slow transformation of how we moved through the world—learning to arrive with curiosity rather than assumptions, to see people rather than scenery, to engage with reality rather than our ideas about reality.

The road from Assisi was teaching us that the sacred wasn't separate from the ordinary—it was hidden within it, waiting to be recognized and honored in the flour on Maria's apron, the photographs in Giuseppe's album, the stories of a village that was never just a stop along the way.

Act IV: In The World and Of The World

"What does the Lord require of you but to do justice, and to love kindness, and to walk humbly with your God?"

—Micah 6:8 "

The spiritual life is not a life before, after, or beyond our everyday existence. No, the spiritual life can only be real when it is lived in the midst of the pains and joys of the here and now."

—Henri Nouwen

The Road Narrows

Franco arrived later than usual that morning—almost 11 a.m. I knew that meant he'd probably already done another pickup before coming to us. We loaded up and I saw the other luggage he was already carrying.

"You've got a big load this morning," I commented.

"Yes, helping a friend," he said. "This is for a group staying in the same city you guys are, so it was easy for me to lend a hand."

As we left the city and headed out onto the highway, Franco glanced over at me. "So this is your last rest day before the final push tomorrow, yes? Smart planning. Save your energy for that last walk with your companions."

"Yeah, I figured I've made it this far. Might as well finish strong."

"You've done well, Jonathan. Better than you give yourself credit for."

I noticed that our conversation carried a different weight than before. We'd fallen into an easy rhythm over these days— his questions drawing out my thinking, my presence somehow giving him permission to speak more freely than perhaps he did with the Germans.

"You know what I like about this group?" he said as we wound through Umbrian hillsides. "You're all building something, but you're each bringing different tools. Wilhelm brings his structure, Thomas his contemplation, Gunter his joy. You bring your questions."

"I'm not sure questions are the same as tools. Mine in particular often seem to reflect more doubt than anything else."

"Questions are the most important tool. Faith cannot exist, much less grow, without the fire of doubt lit under it," Franco said. "Structure without questions becomes rigid. Contemplation without questions becomes escape. Even joy without questions can become blindness. You're all offering each other what you don't have yourselves."

I thought about that as vineyards rolled past the window. "What about you? What do you bring?"

Franco smiled. "I bring the scaffolding. My job is to help you build, then take it down when you're done. Scaffolding isn't the building—it's what helps the building go up."

That thought was still on my mind as we pulled into the parking lot. Franco glanced at the modest building ahead of us. "This one's a little further out in the countryside, one of the more modest accommodations along the trail. Should be very quiet—it's outside of town."

"Quiet is good," I said. "I'm going to use the time to write, get some notes down."

"This is a pretty serious leg of the trail that they're on. Probably noticed that when you looked at the trail map and the elevations. So you've got at least three, maybe four hours. Should be a good window for collecting your thoughts."

I spent the afternoon on a small terrace with my laptop, trying to capture the insights from our conversations. Franco's scaffolding metaphor kept circling back. The question Wilhelm had raised in Assisi about orthodoxy and heresy—I still didn't have a complete answer, but I was beginning to see the shape of one.

I opened ChatGPT and typed out the question that had been nagging at me: how do we think about institutions and orthodoxy when they start protecting themselves instead of serving what they were built for? The conversation that followed helped clarify something I'd been feeling but couldn't quite articulate. Institutions become defensive systems. Scaffolding becomes permanent. The structure becomes more important than what it was meant to support.

I sat back and looked out at the countryside. In two days we'd be in Rome—the ultimate expression of institutional Christianity. The eternal city. The headquarters of scaffolding that had stood for two thousand years. What would Francis have thought, walking these same roads toward that center of power?

When the guys arrived dusty and satisfied from the trail, their energy was different—lighter somehow, like men who'd accomplished something difficult and were proud of it. We cleaned up and gathered for dinner, the conversation easy and warm.

"Tomorrow's our last day of walking," I said. "I'll be joining you."

"Good," Wilhelm said simply.

The next morning, I shouldered my pack with them for the last time. The trail to Piediluco descended through oak forests that occasionally opened onto valley views. We walked mostly in comfortable silence, each of us processing the week in our own way. There was no need to fill the quiet with words. We'd said what needed saying. Now we were just walking together.

Gunter called out from ahead. "Look. See the hawk there?" He gestured upward. We stopped to watch a hawk circling overhead, wings catching the early light. It let out a sharp cry that pierced the morning quiet, then arced and disappeared over the cypress trees.

"I wonder if they viewed hawks differently in Francis's time than we do today?" Thomas said.

"Let's ask ChatGPT," Gunter said.

I pulled out my phone. "We happen to be in a good spot— I've got signal." I typed in the question. "Did medieval people view hawks differently than we do today?"

The response came back quickly. I read it aloud: "Hawks held special significance in medieval bestiaries—books of beasts that were part natural history, part Christian allegory. Each animal carried spiritual meaning. Hawks were seen as messengers between heaven and earth because they could fly high yet still see the terrain below. They symbolized spiritual insight—the kind of vision that comes from being above the situation but still attentive, present, watchful."

"So vision from above, but still attentive below," Gunter said. "Whatever it sees on the ground gets framed by the bigger picture. It can see both the horizon and the mouse."

"Is it too early in the day for a discussion of the tension between transcendence and immanence?" I asked, already suspecting that it probably was. "The top-down versus the bottom-up?"

"It may not be too early," Gunter said. "It depends on if we can talk about it without abstract words like 'immanence.'" He said it with a smirk, suggesting he was glad that he knew what the word meant.

Still a few feet ahead of us, Wilhelm called back without breaking stride, "Yes, it is. Way too early," and kept walking.

We fell silent for a moment, watching the hawk make another wide circle. Then Gunter spoke up.

"You know that story about Francis preaching to the birds? You believe that?"

I thought about it. "Probably. I don't find it difficult to believe at all."

"How so?" Thomas asked.

"Well, it's easy to believe he preached," I said. "The hard thing to believe is—did they understand him?"

Gunter let out a sharp laugh. "Ha! Good one, Jonathan."

Wilhelm, still a few paces ahead, called back without turning around: "Or whether they would do anything about it."

We all stopped walking. Even Gunter looked surprised.

"Wilhelm!" Thomas said, grinning. "Was that a joke?"

"It was an observation," Wilhelm said, but there was the hint of a smile in his voice.

The hawk caught our attention again as it circled back toward us in a long arc. As it got closer, I could just make out its head turning, eyes locked on something. It reminded me that perspective requires not only distance but also the ability to see. In the hawk's case, even from several hundred yards up, it could spot the twitching whiskers of a field mouse. I'd gained plenty of distance from my evangelical past. Sometimes I wondered if it was becoming too much distance—that I was losing the ability to see clearly enough to offer any meaningful critique.

The hawk let out one more cry and banked toward the east, disappearing beyond a line of cypress trees.

We came upon a small stone chapel tucked among the trees—ancient, weathered, with no village or hamlet anywhere near it. We stopped, dropping our packs with synchronized sighs of relief.

"What's this doing out here?" Gunter wondered aloud.

Thomas looked around at the empty forest. "There are so many of these along the pilgrimage trail. We saw it in Assisi too—many dozens of churches and chapels in and around the city."

"Over a thousand in Rome," Wilhelm added.

"In Rome alone? Over a thousand?" I said.

"Actually closer to fifteen hundred," Thomas said. "But yes, far more than we could ever see."

"In America, I'm used to each denomination getting one church in a city—or if it's a big one like the Baptists, maybe two or three," I said. "It's odd to think about Catholicism being the only religion needing so many churches and chapels."

"They are all—"

"Ebenezers," Wilhelm said, completing my sentence.

"Exactly, Wilhelm. I forgot how biblically literate you are."

Gunter looked at him. "Who?"

"Not who—what," Wilhelm said with a slight smile. "Stacking up stones to commemorate something. The Israelites called it an Ebenezer. These chapels are just a more developed form of that same ancient idea—marking places where God made a move."

We stood there looking at the small chapel, imagining the centuries of pilgrims who'd stopped here, the countless prayers whispered inside those walls.

"What are you thinking about?" Thomas asked me, his voice barely above a murmur.

"Tomorrow. Rome. What comes after walking."

He nodded slowly. "The pilgrimage doesn't end when the walking stops. Sometimes it's just beginning."

I thought about Francis making this same journey eight hundred years ago. Walking from Assisi toward Rome, carrying his radical vision of gospel poverty, heading straight into the heart of institutional power to ask permission from the Pope himself to start a new order. What must that have been like? The peasant approaching the palace. The mystic facing the machinery of the church.

"Do you think Francis was nervous?" I asked Thomas. "Approaching Rome to see the Pope?"

Thomas considered. "He was certainly anxious but completely confident at the same time. That's how it works when you're certain of your call but uncertain of your reception."

"Strategic innocence," I said, remembering Franco's phrase.

"Exactly. He knew what he'd experienced was real. He just didn't know if anyone else would see it."

That evening, we packed for the last time, knowing tomorrow Franco would drive us all to Rome together. The walking was done. Whatever came next would be different.

All five of us crowded into Franco's van the next morning for the final leg to Rome. The mood was different than previous drives—something between celebration and solemnity, like we all knew we were crossing a threshold. Even Gunter was quieter than usual, looking out the window as Italian countryside gave way to increasing signs of urbanization.

As Franco navigated the morning traffic, I decided to raise the question that had been forming since Assisi.

"Franco, thinking about our time in Rome ahead—it's got me thinking more about institutions and orthodoxy. How do we know when codes and creeds become more of a limit or a prison than a help?"

Franco glanced in the rearview mirror, then back to the road. "That's the right question for approaching Rome. What's behind it?"

"I've been thinking a lot about where my journey started, with deconstruction, and how the origin of that word is more about the instability and contingency of meaning, the limits of language itself. It implies the boundaries of orthodoxy can only be artificially determined."

Franco nodded slowly. "Let me tell you about Thomas Aquinas—Thomas, with your love of church history, you'll appreciate this. The chief doctor of orthodoxy found those limits himself."

Thomas leaned in and said, "Aquinas—long on analysis, short on mystery."

"Well said, Thomas," Franco replied. "This story addresses that very point." He began in a way that suggested he had told this story many times—he had the cadences and beats just right.

"Aquinas spent his whole life building this massive theological structure—the Summa Theologica, probably the most comprehensive systematic theology ever written. We're talking about three major parts, over three thousand pages, dozens of volumes depending on the edition. He borrowed much of the architecture from Aristotle—all that logic, all those categories. It's beautiful, really. All of Christian doctrine organized into perfect logical categories, every question addressed, every objection answered."

"But?" I prompted, hearing where this might be going.

"But near the end of his life, Aquinas had a life-changing encounter with the Holy Spirit during Mass. Afterward he said: 'All that I have written seems like straw compared to what has now been revealed to me.' He never wrote another word. And this wasn't after completing his masterwork—he was deep into the third part of the Summa, with significant work still ahead of him. He just . . . stopped. Left it unfinished."

The van was completely silent. The comment had really landed with Thomas, who knew the Aquinas well.

"What do you think he saw?" Thomas asked quietly.

Franco was thoughtful for a moment. "I think he finally hit the boundary. After all those years trying to create something perfectly clear, perfectly logical, perfectly complete—he discovered the limits of language itself. All language is abstraction of experience, not the experience itself. And what happened in that Mass was direct experience that couldn't be captured, couldn't be systematized. The Holy Spirit reminded him that words only point toward reality, they never contain it."

I felt something click. I was beginning to get a clearer sense now how truth might transcend language itself.

"His work was brilliant, however limited it might have been looking through a medieval lens before the age of science," Franco said. "But it was still just language trying to describe what can only be experienced. He'd spent decades refining theological language to its highest form, and then he had an encounter that showed him—this is what all the words are pointing toward, but the words themselves can never get you there."

I glanced at Wilhelm and saw a look of concern on his face, eyebrows knitted together. "Sounds interesting, but I can't escape the feeling that we're skating on thin ice. Flirting with something like anarchy."

"I get it. Hard things," Franco said. "Just sit with it. It may make more sense to you later.

"The walls of orthodoxy crack," Franco said slowly, "when they're shaken by the earthquake of direct encounter. Francis knew that. Aquinas learned it. The question for each of you is what will happen when your earthquake comes."

We drove in silence for a while, each of us sitting with that question. The landscape outside had changed completely now—no more rural hillsides, but the sprawl of a major city. We were entering Rome's gravitational field.

Then Franco asked, "So what are you each carrying into Rome? Wilhelm, you start."

Wilhelm, sitting behind Franco, considered carefully. "A renewed appreciation for structure that knows its place."

"Given our discussions about the limits of codes and creeds, that's a wise place to have ended up," Franco said.

"Thomas?" He glanced in the rearview mirror, seeing Thomas's small frame perched in the middle of the backseat—because he was the smallest of the three of us, he always got assigned to the middle seat.

"Questions about whether institutions can preserve mystery without trying to control it."

"Gunter?"

"Joy. And maybe some mischief." He grinned, and we all laughed.

"Don't underestimate that," Franco said. "Joy is subversive in places that take themselves too seriously."

Franco glanced over at me in the passenger seat. "Jonathan?"

"That God didn't build a finished universe. That we're responsible for co-creating it with him."

Franco was quiet for a moment, then nodded slowly. "Now that's what Rome needs to hear. Francis would approve."

I thought about Francis again, making this same approach to Rome. Carrying his unfinished vision, his radical commitment, his questions about what the church could become. Walking straight into the center of power with nothing but his conviction and his companions.

"Franco," I said, "what do you think Francis was feeling as he approached Rome?"

Franco was quiet for a moment, navigating a tricky merge. "I think he was terrified," he finally said. "Not of the Pope, but of what success might mean. If the church accepted his vision, it would have to become institutional. The scaffolding would go up. And he knew—he must have known—that the scaffolding might eventually obscure the very thing he was trying to build."

"But he came anyway," Thomas said.

"He came anyway," Franco agreed. "Because the alternative was letting his vision die with him. Better to risk institutionalization than to refuse to share what he'd discovered."

The city appeared more fully now—ancient and modern mixed together, urban density pressing in from all sides. Then suddenly, St. Peter's dome rising above it all.

Wilhelm pulled out his phone. "I'm checking Google Maps. Our apartment is only two blocks from St. Peter's Square. Franco, why don't you drop us there and we'll walk the rest of the way?"

"Geographic center," Franco said as we got closer. "Spiritual Ground Zero of the Roman Catholic world."

We were approaching St. Peter's Square now, and even from the van I could see the massive scale of it. Gunter, Thomas, and I—the only ones who'd never been to Rome before—pressed closer to the windows.

"This is so much bigger than I imagined," I said. "Those columns look like—"

"Bernini's columns," Franco finished my sentence. "Like two big arms reaching out to embrace the entire square."

We pulled up to the edge of the square, already quite busy with tourists and pilgrims. Franco helped us unload our packs, his movements slower than usual.

"It's a bit overwhelming at first," Franco said. "But you'll get your bearings. I've seen plenty of pilgrimage groups. Most spend their final days either arguing theology or avoiding it entirely. You're demonstrating strategic innocence without even realizing it. Each of you is contributing what you see clearly while remaining open to what the others bring. Rome will be interesting for you."

We stood at the edge of the massive piazza, packs at our feet, and watched Franco drive away. Before us stretched Bernini's colonnade embracing the square, and beyond it, the dome Michelangelo had designed rising into the Roman sky. The road had narrowed to this moment, this arrival, this beginning.

We shouldered our packs and walked the two blocks to our apartment, pilgrims entering the eternal city.

The Power of Presence

Our Roman apartment sat just three blocks from the Vatican, close enough that the bells of St. Peter's became our morning alarm. After settling in and sharing a quick breakfast of coffee and cornetti, Thomas checked his watch.

"If we leave now, we can beat the tour groups."

Wilhelm was already folding his map. "The basilica opens at seven. We could be inside before the crowds arrive."

We walked the three blocks past cafés setting out their morning tables, past shopkeepers hosing down cobblestones, past an elderly priest walking his small dog. Rome stirring into another day, as it had for centuries. As we slipped through an arched gate along the papal escape wall, Bernini's colonnade opened before us like a mother's arms.

Gunter stopped walking entirely. "Incredible. Look at this place."

The square stretched before us like a stone ocean, the Egyptian obelisk rising from its center. A handful of early pilgrims were already gathering, but nothing like the crush that would come later.

Thomas walked slowly toward the center. "I'm trying to imagine Francis here. A twenty-eight-year-old merchant's son from a backwater town, approaching all this accumulated power."

"With nothing but conviction and eleven ragged followers," Wilhelm added.

"This obelisk has been here since Caligula brought it from Egypt," I said. "Francis would have seen its shadow in a very different Rome—perhaps thirty thousand people where there had once been a million. The grand basilica and square we see today were just dreams."

Gunter gestured toward the massive façade. "You know what's ironic? This whole project's enormous cost led to aggressive indulgence sales, which sparked the Protestant Reformation when Luther protested in 1517. The Reformation was actually sparked by an over-budget construction project."

"A ghost town with delusions of grandeur," Thomas said with uncharacteristic sharpness. "Rather like institutions in general—maintaining impressive facades while the life inside slowly drains away."

The line at the security checkpoint was mercifully short. Within twenty minutes, we had passed through and stood at the entrance to St. Peter's Basilica.

Nothing prepares you for the scale. I had seen photographs, watched documentaries, read descriptions—but stepping through those doors, the sheer immensity of the space overwhelmed every expectation. The nave stretched before us like a canyon of marble and gold, two football fields to the distant altar where Bernini's baldachin rose beneath Michelangelo's dome.

Most visitors were already drifting toward that distant spectacle, but Thomas touched my arm. "This way first," he said, steering us to the right. "The crowds always head straight down the middle. Let's start at the edges."

We followed him into a chapel just off the entrance, and there she was—Michelangelo's Pietà, protected now behind glass since a madman attacked it with a hammer in 1972. Mary cradling her dead son—the marble so polished it seemed to glow from within. She looked impossibly young, younger than her son, and I remembered reading that Michelangelo had explained this by saying that perfect purity preserves youth. Whatever the theology, the sculpture stopped us cold. Here was grief rendered eternal, suffering transformed into beauty without diminishing its weight.

"He carved this when he was twenty-four," Wilhelm said quietly. "The same age as Francis when he kissed the leper."

Gunter shook his head in wonder. "Twenty-four. It's humbling how much brilliant work gets done by people that age. Bob Dylan wrote 'Blowin' in the Wind' at twenty-one. Steve Jobs started Apple at twenty-one." He glanced at me. "What were we doing at twenty-four?"

"Not carving masterpieces," I admitted.

Wilhelm smiled. "Don't forget Einstein—twenty-six when he published relativity. And your beloved Beatles were barely out of their teens when they changed music forever."

We moved deeper into the basilica, making our way toward the crossing where the transept meets the nave. Here Bernini's baldachin rose above the papal altar—ninety-five feet of twisted bronze columns marking the spot directly above St. Peter's tomb. The bronze had been stripped from the Pantheon's portico to build it, a fact that reminded me how empires cannibalize their predecessors.

"Four times the height of my apartment building," Wilhelm murmured, his engineer's mind running calculations. "And it's dwarfed by the dome above it."

Michelangelo's dome soared overhead, light streaming through windows at its base, the interior covered with mosaics depicting Christ, Mary, and ranks of saints ascending toward heaven. I craned my neck until it ached. The words around the base of the dome were visible even from the floor: Tu es Petrus— "You are Peter, and upon this rock I will build my church."

"You know what I read?" I said, still gazing upward. "Michelangelo took over as chief architect here when he was seventy-one. Our age. He never saw it finished, but that—" I gestured at the soaring vault—"that was his final vision."

"So there's hope for us yet," Wilhelm said drily.

Thomas had drifted toward a side chapel where an elderly Italian woman knelt in prayer, her lips moving silently. "Look at her face," he whispered when we joined him. "She's not seeing institutional power. She's encountering presence."

Gunter stood before the bronze statue of St. Peter, its foot worn smooth by centuries of pilgrims' kisses and touches. "Every step in this place is an act of submission," he observed. "The architecture is designed to make you feel small. And yet—" he paused, watching the old woman pray.

For my part, I found myself overwhelmed by the sheer accumulation of devotion the space represented. Centuries of pilgrims, centuries of prayers, centuries of both genuine faith and institutional manipulation layered into the very stones. How do you receive this kind of beauty without being broken by the power claims it's designed to support?

"Strategic innocence," I murmured to Wilhelm. "Francis must have wrestled with exactly this question."

"Maybe you appreciate the artistry while questioning the authority," he replied. "Love the gift, resist the giver's claims about what the gift means."

We emerged from the basilica nearly two hours later, blinking in the late morning sun. The square had transformed—tour groups everywhere now, guides holding colored flags aloft, the hum of a dozen languages filling the space that had been so quiet at dawn.

"I need to process that," Thomas said. "I think I'll walk. Watch people for a while."

"I passed a market on our way here," Wilhelm said. "I thought I might shop for dinner, spend the afternoon cooking. My grandmother always said the meal is where the day comes together."

Gunter had been studying his map. "There's something I want to see. The Pyramid of Cestius—and the Protestant Cemetery beside it. Keats is buried there."

We agreed to reconvene at the apartment for dinner, then dispersed into Rome.

As my companions headed their separate ways, I found myself drawn toward the Tiber, following the ancient river toward Castel Sant'Angelo. Frustrated with my guidebook's scattered information, I stopped walking. Wait—I could use ChatGPT for this.

"Tell me about Castel Sant'Angelo," I asked the AI. "Not just facts, but what makes it historically significant."

The response revealed layers I hadn't expected: Built as Hadrian's mausoleum, it became Rome's most formidable prison. The 800-meter fortified corridor called the Passetto di Borgo runs directly from the papal apartments to the castle. When Rome was sacked in 1527, Pope Clement VII fled along this passage.

The image struck me—the Vicar of Christ sprinting nearly nine football fields, papal robes billowing, as imperial soldiers ransacked St. Peter's below.

As I walked back up the bank of the Tiber towards Castel Sant'Angelo, I heard the music. Faint at first, but it was coming from a busker sitting at the base of one of the massive castle walls, playing "Wonderwall" by Oasis. It seemed an odd juxtaposition—the walls of a fortress that had imprisoned so many, while someone sang "you're gonna be the one that saves me."

I approached closer. As I got nearer, I could tell he was quite good. I should tip him well. I dropped a few euros into his guitar case. He noticed me hanging out longer than most—the majority just stopped for a moment and continued walking. When he got to the end of the song, we struck up a conversation.

Turns out he was British, which explained the Oasis selection. A gap-year traveler, he told me, who'd taken the gap year five years ago and never gone back.

"Who are your influences?" he asked. "Favorite singer-songwriters?"

"You probably haven't heard of them. Before your time."

He gave me a look. "Try me."

"Jackson Browne. James Taylor."

"I'm young, not ignorant," he said with a grin. "Any song-writer worth the name knows those two. Most of us would kill to write just one song as good as their worst."

"Taking a break," he said, leaning his guitar up against the castle wall. "You play?"

"I'm a singer-songwriter." Even as the words were leaving my mouth I knew it was an overstatement. "Well, I used to be anyway. But this time in Italy has inspired me. I'm working on a new one."

"If you don't mind, could I hear some of it?"

"Not quite ready for that, I think." I looked longingly at the guitar leaning against the wall. "What would be great, though—I think I might be able to pull some of it together if I just had a gui-tar to work with. I haven't touched mine for three weeks. I miss it."

"You could use mine," he said. "I'm on break for the next fifteen minutes."

"You trust me with it?"

"It's road-tested, don't worry. If I'm comfortable leaning it against this big stone wall, I'm not too worried about what might happen if you get to cradle it for a few minutes."

I picked up his guitar, feeling the familiar weight, the worn frets under my fingers. I was glad that it was a classical guitar—nylon strings were much easier on the fingertips. The neck was a little wider, but I could adapt to that. I began trying out the verses and the beginning of the chorus that had come to me in Assisi: You're not broken, the fire's still smokin' . . .

That morning on the walk along the Tiber, I'd been working on the next piece, and now it seemed to fall together pretty quickly. To pair with the opening line I had come up with, And a little wind might make it roar. And then I finish the couplet with: Bread is broken, you've awoken, now go and find an open door. The communion reference felt important.

It took only two or three passes of singing it for the pieces to click into place. The busker smiled and said, "That's quite good, old man."

"Perhaps it will be when it's finished," I said.

I handed back his guitar, shook his hand, and headed back to meet up with the other guys.

As I left the castle heading back along the Tiber, I decided to cross over on Ponte Sant'Angelo—the Bridge of Angels. Built by Emperor Hadrian over 1,000 years ago when bishops were still outlaws, long before they came to rule the empire. The bridge's remarkable angel statues were added much later by Bernini, the same artist who designed the colonnade around St. Peter's Square.

So in the company of these stone angels I continued across the bridge singing the new chorus just under my breath.

You're not broken, the fire is still smoking, a little wind could make it roar.

Bread's been broken, you've awoken. Now going to find an open door.

I particularly liked the bluesy feel. I didn't have much choice. No matter how creative I tried to be, my love of the pentatonic scale kept pulling me back to the blues.

When we reconvened for dinner that evening, Wilhelm had transformed our apartment into something approaching domestic perfection.

"Proper Roman domestic life," he announced with satisfaction. "My grandmother taught me that meals should be simple ingredients treated with respect, everyone gathered, no rushing."

As we settled into our seats, the wine began to flow and so did the stories of how each of us had spent the afternoon.

Wilhelm gestured toward the kitchen with quiet satisfaction. "While you were all wandering, I found the market. Fresh tomatoes, basil, proper olive oil." He had spent the afternoon shopping for ingredients and reading in the apartment, and the results were on the table before us. "My grandmother always said the meal is where the day comes together. I wanted to make sure we had a proper place to land."

Gunter leaned back in his chair. "I took the metro out to the Pyramid of Cestius—you know there's an actual ancient Egyptian-style pyramid right here in Rome? Built for some wealthy Roman two thousand years ago." He swirled his wine. "But what struck me was the cemetery beside it. The Protestant Cemetery, they call it. Keats is buried there. Shelley's ashes too." He paused. "I stood at Keats's grave—he died at twenty-five, younger than my sons. His epitaph says, 'Here lies one whose name was writ in water.' All that genius, and he died thinking he'd be forgotten." Gunter shook his head slowly. "Two centuries later, strangers still come from around the world to stand at his grave. Sometimes the water holds the name after all."

Thomas had been quiet, but now he spoke. "I spent most of my time watching people. At the Trevi, at the Spanish Steps. Couples mostly." He stirred his wine thoughtfully. "In my work, I see so many relationships that have calcified—people going through motions, performing intimacy without actually connecting. But today I watched strangers share genuine moments of awe. A Japanese couple and an Italian family, neither speaking the other's language, helping each other take photos. Shared wonder as a kind of universal grammar."

I told them about the busker, the borrowed guitar, the song finally clicking into place. "Something about playing music against those ancient walls," I said. "It felt like joining a conversation that's been going on for centuries."

"Speaking of things that last," Thomas said, "it's remarkable how solid these Roman structures still are."

Wilhelm's engineering mind engaged. "Volcanic ash, lime, seawater. Over time the crystal structure heals—it reinforces itself. Our concrete tires; theirs matures."

"Francis built with fragile materials—poverty, joy, humility, song," I said. "Under pressure they didn't crack; they set."

I shared my experience with the AI companion. "It was like having a knowledgeable friend who could point out connections across centuries."

"Just as Rome made everything Roman," Wilhelm observed, "we make everything American."

"Every empire calls itself different," Thomas said.

Wilhelm set down his wine glass. "Francis didn't reject imperial power. He found a way to engage it that neither legitimized its claims to absolute authority nor dismissed its genuine achievements."

Thomas raised his glass. "To building something that might outlast our empires."

The Romans learned to make stone that matures under stress. Francis did the same with poverty, joy, and humility. Our glasses clicked; beyond the shutters, the bells began again.

Tomorrow we would venture into the heart of the institution itself—the Vatican Museums, the Sistine Chapel. But for now, Rome had given us exactly what we needed: a day to practice presence before confronting power.

The Ceiling Between Worlds

We had taken a little longer than planned at breakfast. Since the Vatican Museums were only a few blocks away, no one seemed in a hurry. The room was bright with late-morning light, the quiet clatter of cups, the faint hiss of milk frothing behind the bar.

Thomas was the first to speak. "So, the Vatican Museums," he said, setting down his spoon. "I'm conflicted."

"Conflicted? Why?" Gunter asked, pulling on his jacket.

"I know what you mean," I said. "I'm feeling some of the same."

Thomas nodded. "It's not about the beauty of the artifacts themselves. It's about the power and coercion behind how they were acquired."

"But can't we judge the art on its own terms?" Gunter asked. "The beauty exists independent of its origins." He turned to Wilhelm. "Don't you agree?"

Wilhelm raised an eyebrow, his expression suggesting mild bewilderment at why we found such discussions important. "I choose not to traffic in such abstractions," he said. "The art is here. We are here. That seems sufficient."

Thomas smiled. "Compartmentalization can be a useful coping strategy. If I think too long about the politics and exploitation behind all this art, I lose the ability to enjoy it." He paused, looking into his coffee. "My grandfather collected African masks—beautiful pieces he bought from a dealer in Amsterdam. When I was twelve, I learned they'd been looted from villages during the Congo occupation. I loved those masks. Still do. But I can't look at them without seeing the hands they were stolen from."

The table went quiet for a moment.

"Didn't seem to bother you so much when we were at the Uffizi," Wilhelm observed gently.

"That was different," Thomas said. "The Medicis bought power through patronage. The popes ruled by divine right. Hypocrisy feels more sacred here."

Gunter laughed. "Sacred hypocrisy. There's a phrase that belongs in a theology textbook."

I smiled, but the comment stayed with me. The last time I'd entered a great museum, in Florence, I was still measuring faith in propositions and beauty in mastery—how the artist bent light and color to his will. Today, after two weeks of walking, I suspected beauty wasn't about mastery at all. It was about coherence—the ordering of things by love rather than control.

That shift had been creeping up on me since the morning Wilhelm and I walked through the pre-dawn darkness outside Assisi, when the world felt less like a collection of objects to be understood and more like a living conversation I was joining. It deepened when Franco first appeared on the path, speaking of emergence rather than explanation. And it crystallized in the Porziuncola, standing in that tiny chapel where Francis chose smallness over grandeur—not as rejection of beauty, but as a different understanding of what beauty serves. Beauty, I was beginning to see, wasn't about control or possession. It was about coherence—love making visible what was always meant to be.

We left the hotel and joined the line that stretched along the Vatican walls. Tour groups formed in clusters like small congregations. The street smelled faintly of espresso and car exhaust.

Thomas looked at the crowd and said, "Every masterpiece in there tells two stories, doesn't it? The story of the art itself—and the story of how it was acquired."

"Papal armies claiming spoils," Gunter said. "Noble families buying divine favor. Colonial expeditions bringing home trophies."

"But doesn't beauty transcend its origins?" Wilhelm countered. "These works are preserved, protected, shared. Whatever their beginnings, they serve another purpose now."

Francis had never rejected beauty or culture. He had simply insisted they be ordered by love rather than by power.

"The real question," Thomas said, "is whether such beauty justifies its price. Can transcendent art redeem the violence of its collection?"

No one answered. The bells of St. Peter's echoed overhead, rolling like distant surf across the city.

Inside, the first impression was abundance—corridors of human imagination spilling into one another like tributaries of a single river. Masterpieces that would anchor entire museums elsewhere were here reduced to hallway decoration.

In the Museum of Classical Antiquities, rows of marble emperors gazed across the room, their eyes sightless but still commanding. A massive bust of Augustus dominated one corner, his expression of absolute calm the very image of power frozen into stone.

Thomas paused before a sarcophagus. "Each of these pieces whispers the same question," he said. "Who paid for this? What conquest made it possible?"

"What villages could have been fed with the gold leaf in just this room?" Gunter added quietly.

Wilhelm ran his fingers along a plinth. "The scale of accumulation," he began, then stopped, surprised by his own tone.

"Hold on," I said gently. "If we see only what's broken, we'll miss what's been redeemed. Otherwise, all we'll find here are shadows."

Thomas studied a statue of Venus. "Perhaps beauty itself redeems the intent," he said. "It isn't baptized by possession—only by purpose."

Wilhelm nodded toward the emperor's likeness. "Power creates the conditions for beauty, but beauty judges power. Augustus ruled the world, but he needed Virgil to make him immortal."

We walked on. In the Raphael Rooms, theology and humanism danced together in color and light. In The School of Athens, Plato pointed upward, Aristotle downward—the eternal argument suspended in perfect symmetry.

"How meaningful is it," I asked, "that the subject matter of these works was chosen more by the patron's purse than by the artist's imagination?"

Thomas chuckled. "No different from cinema today. The producer shapes the message more than the director."

"Raphael worked for two popes," I said. "Julius II—the warrior pope—wanted knowledge to serve authority. Leo X—the Medici—wanted culture to civilize faith. Between them you can trace the shift from command to imagination."

The air smelled faintly of varnish and age. A docent's voice drifted through the gallery in German, reciting facts about pigment and composition.

We passed into the Gallery of Maps. Italy stretched in painted relief across the walls, the known world of the sixteenth century rendered in lapis and gold.

"Look at the precision," Wilhelm said. "Every province exact to its neighbor."

"But look what's being mapped," Thomas replied. "Territories, yes—but also souls. These are missionary boundaries disguised as geography."

We moved on to tapestry. Gold thread glimmered under the soft lighting, woven into scenes of gospel tenderness.

"Took a team of weavers a year to make one of these," Wilhelm murmured.

"Gold worth more than villages," Thomas replied.

Wilhelm studied the edge of one tapestry, his voice softening. "Someone believed this beauty would outlast them."

I looked at the shimmer of gold bordering Jesus' robe. "Gold edging poverty," I said. "It could be hypocrisy—or sacrament."

Thomas looked up from his guidebook. "And today?"

"Today it feels like sacrament," I said.

We were quiet for a while. It struck me that the popes had gathered not just art but the story of aspiration itself—the human longing to translate wonder into form. Maybe that's why we still come: not to admire power, but to remember what beauty looks like when it outlives the hands that claimed it.

The crowd thickened as we neared the Sistine Chapel. The air grew close, the murmur of languages blending into a low hum. The guards spoke in ritual cadence: Silenzio, per favore. No photographs.

The chapel held us like a tide pool—bodies pressed and swirling in slow currents. Tour groups eddied around their guides' raised umbrellas while individuals drifted between larger flows. I could feel the heat from the people beside me, smell the mix of perfume, sweat, and reverence. Children whined in French, teenagers whispered in Spanish, and underneath it all a low murmur of prayer in tongues I couldn't identify—humanity breathing beneath a painted heaven.

But there was another current, vertical rather than horizontal. The ceiling pulled every gaze upward like reverse gravity. Even those rushing through found themselves stopped, necks craning, caught by something that refused to let go.

My neck began to ache. I looked down to massage the cramp, and that's when I saw him. Franco stood just beyond a clutch of tourists, perfectly still, the crowd flowing around him like water around a stone. He was studying the space between God and Adam—the fingertip gap where everything begins.

I pressed through the crowd toward him. An elderly woman fingering worn rosary beads created an eddy I had to navigate around. When I finally reached him, Franco didn't turn but somehow knew I was there.

"Can you see the anticipation?" he asked softly. "What do you think Adam felt as he saw the approaching hand?"

"Maybe wonder," I said. "Or fear—the moment before everything changes."

"Yes," he said. "But look closer—Adam's hand is already reaching back. Creation participating in its own becoming. The universe isn't finished, Jonathan. It's still reaching, still becoming."

I followed his gaze. "Teilhard called that complexification, didn't he? Creation moving toward greater unity?"

Franco nodded. "Yes, though complexification can sound mechanical, as if describing gears. I prefer another phrase: emergent coherence. At a certain level of relational complexity, something new comes into being—something more than the sum of what preceded it."

He turned toward me, eyes bright. "Think musically: single notes forming chords, chords into melody, melodies woven into song, songs layered into symphony. Each level gives birth to something that wasn't possible before, yet carries the essence of all that came before."

He gestured upward again. "Or in painting: color blending into tone, tone into form, form into composition and light.

What emerges isn't just complexity—it's coherence. Beauty is coherence made visible."

The words seemed to vibrate in the air. "So beauty isn't decorative," I said quietly. "It's revelatory."

"Yes," Franco whispered. "The pattern of love itself made manifest. The Church preserved beauty, even when it misunderstood it. These walls are filled with proof that love keeps finding ways to cohere through the ruins of power."

We stood there in silence, necks aching, eyes lifted. The crowd pressed and murmured below us, but we were elsewhere—caught between two worlds.

Franco's voice dropped to a whisper. "That space between the fingers—both infinite and infinitesimal—it holds everything that matters about love and longing."

For a breath, nothing moved. Then a guard's polite hand on my shoulder urged me forward. I turned to respond—and Franco was gone. The crowd had swallowed the space where he'd stood, but the air there felt different somehow, cooler, like the moment after lightning when the atmosphere hasn't yet settled back into itself. I caught the faint scent of something I couldn't name—not incense exactly, but something older, like the smell of stone after rain.

Outside the Vatican Museums, the afternoon light felt sharp after the marble coolness. The others joined me at the base of the steps.

"That was extraordinary," Thomas said quietly.

Gunter stretched his back. "And exhausting—but worth every step."

Wilhelm smiled faintly. "That's the mark of greatness—you always leave wanting one more look."

We lingered for a moment before turning toward our hotel. The wall of the Vatican rose beside us, ancient stone declaring permanence. I thought of Franco's words, of coherence, of beauty that outlives power. Francis had found a way beneath walls like these—not through force, but through grace. I realized the harder pilgrimage was never through the hills or the halls of power, but through the walls within myself—those still waiting for love to find the door.

The sun was warm on my face. Somewhere in the distance, church bells marked the hour. Tomorrow we would leave Rome. But first, there was one more conversation I needed to have—not with Franco this time, but with myself.

Thunder Road

Sunday was our last full day in Rome. We slept in, still processing the theological weight of our Vatican Museums journey the day before, knowing that the evening's Springsteen concert would keep us up even later. A restlessness had been building since Franco's mysterious disappearance in the Sistine Chapel. His final words about love breeding trust and the imagination learning to dance kept circling in my mind, feeling both complete and unfinished, like a song missing its final verse.

I was hoping to hear "Thunder Road," one of my Springsteen favorites. That song would crown our pilgrimage perfectly—its line, "The door's open but the ride ain't free," resonating deeply with everything we'd discovered about transformation requiring both invitation and sacrifice.

After weeks of walking through Umbrian hills, learning about strategic innocence and non-coercive love, I had come to understand that pilgrimage isn't about destinations but about embracing uncertainties and challenges along the way.

Over coffee, we discussed our plan for the day: walking to Saint Peter's Square to hear the pope's noon Angelus prayer. Throughout our pilgrimage, we had joked about receiving blessings from both the "boss" of the Church and the "boss" of American music. But that lighthearted jest had evolved into earnest conversation about how deeply Pope Francis embodied the spirit of his namesake Saint Francis.

Thomas stirred his espresso thoughtfully. "Both Francises approached power the same way—not to destroy it or be co-opted by it, but to transform it through witness."

Wilhelm, spreading jam on his cornetto with characteristic precision, looked skeptical. "But institutional change requires more than symbolic gestures. Systems have their own momentum."

"Maybe that's exactly the point," Gunter said. "Both Francises understood that you can't force institutional trans-formation. You can only model it and trust others to recognize what they're seeing."

As we waited for the Angelus to begin, I found myself think-ing about the thousands who had gathered. As noon approached, the late May sun drew sweat from our foreheads. A breeze occa-sionally swept across the square, carrying a hint of sea salt from the Mediterranean fifteen miles away.

We sought refuge beneath the shade of one of Bernini's massive columns—one of 284 towering structures encasing the square. Leaning against the cool stone, I found myself wrestling with the conflicted history etched into these monuments. The columns had been erected in the aftermath of Europe's Thirty Years' War, when Catholics and Protestants had slaughtered each other with religious fervor. Yet perhaps the Roman Church saw them as a way to restore order and spiritual purpose in a world reeling from calamity.

While waiting, we found ourselves debating Pope Francis's legacy.

Wilhelm grumbled. "Symbolic gestures are all well and good, but they hardly suffice to reform an institution as ancient and entrenched as the Roman Church."

"But doesn't that prove the power of strategic innocence?" I interjected. "Like his namesake, Pope Francis isn't trying to destroy the system from outside. He's transforming it from within through embodied witness."

Gunter leaned in. "Did not Saint Francis himself begin with symbolic gestures—embracing the leper, stripping naked in the town square?"

Thomas spoke calmly. "Perhaps concrete change isn't the most crucial element. Francis's model of simplicity and his efforts to strip away the distractions of wealth are fundamentally healthy for the spiritual life of the Church."

"Pope Francis approaches even his critics as human beings rather than institutional roles," I said. "That's exactly what his namesake did with Pope Innocent III—he saw a person, not just a position."

When Francis finally stepped into the window of his suite, a cheer arose from the gathered faithful. From that elevated perch, a football field's distance away, I wondered whether we all looked as small to him as he did to us.

His voice was unexpectedly musical as he offered his brief homily. There was something deeply edifying about 70,000 strangers standing together as one.

What struck me most was Wilhelm's reaction. His usual critical analysis had given way to something softer. When the Pope raised his hand in blessing, Wilhelm removed his cap—a small gesture that revealed more than any of his arguments had.

After our Vatican adventures and a bit more sightseeing, we headed back to our apartment for a break before the concert that night. As we collapsed into chairs in our common room, the question arose.

"How long do we have before we need to head out?" Thomas asked, checking his watch.

"We don't need to be there for the opening act," Gunter suggested. "We don't even know who they are. Better to save our energy for staying through the end—which will run hours past what our bedtimes have been."

Wilhelm shifted in his chair. "Gentlemen, this is our last full day in Rome. I choose not to spend it sleeping."

"Wilhelm," I said, "we're all pushing seventy. We've earned the right to a strategic nap."

Thomas looked between us, then said quietly, "What if we arrive maybe an hour before the opening act? We'd get better field position to actually see the stage, but still have time to rest."

Wilhelm stood, straightening his shirt. "You gentlemen enjoy your rest. I'm going to visit the Baths of Caracalla—the southwestern section has some fascinating examples of Roman hypocaust heating systems." I suspected he used the technical term just to show he'd done his homework carefully.

We looked at each other after he left. None of us had any idea what hypocaust heating was, and we weren't about to find out.

Two hours later, Wilhelm was back, announcing his entrance with a slight air of self-satisfaction that he'd been strong enough to keep walking while we slept.

"Gentlemen," he said, checking his watch. "Time to depart. We should leave now if we want reasonable positioning."

Post-nap and somewhat refreshed, we set out from our apartment with pre-concert adrenaline convincing us we could walk the entire distance to Circus Maximus.

"How far is it actually?" I asked as we stood outside our building, debating whether to walk or grab a taxi.

"Just three kilometers," Gunter said confidently.

"Two miles," Wilhelm added for my benefit, "for the metrically challenged American." He smiled. "That's only a fraction of what we've been walking every day."

"Well, not all of us," I said, thinking of the days I'd ridden with Franco while they tackled the mountain stages.

Gunter waved off the concern. "I think we can make it. Let's give it a go. We're pilgrims, after all."

Half a mile in, reality set in—our pilgrimage-weary legs protesting, the distance suddenly seeming to triple. Two weeks of mountain trails and Roman cobblestones had accumulated in our muscles like compound interest. What might have been manageable on fresh legs now felt impossible.

"This is madness," Wilhelm said, already flagging despite his earlier confidence about not needing rest. "We'll be exhausted before we even arrive."

We spotted a taxi and flagged it down, then immediately be-gan debating whether it was wise—the roads closer to the venue would surely be jammed with 70,000 converging fans.

The driver—wearing a vintage Born to Run tour shirt—stepped out as he heard us arguing. "No problem, no problem!" he said in English, waving us in. "I get you there, trust me."

As we settled in, he asked where we were from, how long we'd been Springsteen fans. Before we could fully answer, he'd tuned his stereo to the SiriusXM Springsteen channel. "Born to Run" was just beginning—the opening harmonica making us all grin at the synchronicity.

As we got closer to the venue and began encountering streams of people heading the same direction, he turned to us. "You want windows down? Pick up the vibe, yes?"

The evening air was cool and perfect. We rolled them down and immediately the energy changed—snatches of singing from the sidewalks, laughter, that familiar anticipatory buzz I remem-bered from revival meetings. Groups of Italians practiced the chorus to "Badlands" in heavily accented English. Aging rock-ers in vintage tour shirts converged with young Romans who'd grown up on their parents' albums.

"You see?" our driver said, grinning in the rearview mirror as we crawled through the increasingly dense crowd. "The Boss—he brings everyone together."

As we descended toward the ancient chariot-racing grounds, the venue revealed itself gradually—massive stage scaffolding where emperors once sat, modern sound towers rising from stones that had heard the roar of ancient crowds. Our driver managed to get us surprisingly close before the human density made it impossible to continue.

"Here—this is good," he said, refusing our attempts to tip extra. "No, no—we are all going to church tonight, yes? The church of rock and roll!"

As we joined the river of people flowing toward the entrance, seventy thousand people were becoming one body, and we were cells being drawn into something larger than ourselves.

The taxi ride had given us time to process the day. "Watching that blessing," Thomas said as we walked, "I realized I've been approaching faith too intellectually. Sometimes you just need to receive what's being offered."

Wilhelm nodded. "You know what struck me? The Pope wasn't performing authority—he was offering it."

Passing nearby ancient structures, I thought of all who had crossed these same stones—legionaries, grain carts, prisoners, and now concert-goers. Constantine had claimed to see a vision at the Milvian Bridge: "In this sign, conquer." Tonight, these same ancient roads would carry us toward something differ-ent—not conquest but communion.

Entering the Circus Maximus, we could hear the pre-show ritual—shouts, laughter, stories of concerts past. But beneath the familiar atmosphere, something else stirred—all the ques-tions and insights from our pilgrimage seemed to be gathering for some kind of resolution I couldn't yet name.

What stirred was hope—hope found not in the commands of some sectarian official, but in the communal presence of oth-ers and mystery made audible. Music, at its most transcendent, is revelation drawing us out of ourselves into a mystical space where bodies, hearts, and breath resonate in mutual longing.

When Bruce took the stage, the energy was immediate. I'd learned he was seventy-three, five years my senior. He was born on September 23, the same birthday as my wife—small convergences that might carry meaning.

It was during "Badlands" that I felt the first tug at my soul. As 70,000 voices joined—"Let the broken hearts stand as the price you've gotta pay"—something inside me began to shift.

All the broken places in my faith, all the theological certainties that had crumbled—suddenly it felt not like loss but like payment for something valuable.

While "Badlands'" final crescendo still hung in the air, Bruce slipped his harmonica brace over his head. It took only three notes for the audience to recognize "Thunder Road." By the second line, so many had joined that Bruce moved away from the mic, conducting an orchestra of souls.

Between and beneath the harmonies, something beyond music welled up in me. The Holy Spirit was at work, not needing sanctuary for space nor pulpit for voice. The chorus of thousands had become a congregation, and soaring within me for the first time in years was a hallelujah—not shouted, but trembling under my breath.

All the pieces from our pilgrimage—Franco's teachings about strategic innocence, Francis's approach to power, the consciousness-as-network insights—suddenly they weren't separate ideas but facets of a single reality I was experiencing.

Just then, I felt someone leaning against me. I turned and was surprised to see Franco staring at me directly—and smiling.

"Franco!" I called over the music. How was he here? He'd vanished from the Sistine Chapel, and now, in a crowd of 70,000, he'd found me.

Franco's eyes conveyed knowledge that needed no definition. "Welcome, pilgrim!" he said. "Funny how Spirit prefers a crowd to a pulpit, isn't it?"

Turning back toward the stage, he concluded, "Not all churches have steeples. Some have scaffolding and sound checks. But the Presence—it still finds a way in."

The crowd swelled with the music, and when I looked again Franco was gone.

As Thunder Road built to its climax—"The door is open but the ride ain't free"—what a fitting summary of this pilgrimage. Without humility nothing opens up; it is the key for opening all the most important doors.

The ancient stones of the Circus Maximus had witnessed gladiators and chariots, imperial spectacles designed to demonstrate power through domination. Tonight, those same stones bore witness to a different kind of gathering—where thousands of individual voices became one song.

Standing there, tears streaming down my face, I felt something fundamental complete itself. Not answers, exactly, but something better: the direct experience of what we'd been talking about all along.

The ride wasn't free—it had cost me certainty, comfort, the security of knowing exactly what I believed. But what I'd received in return was this: the ability to recognize the sacred in a Springsteen concert, to understand that the Spirit uses music to knit us together, creating something larger than any individual could imagine alone.

The next morning came too quickly. My packing ran into the same problem I had at home—too little space for my clothes and the souvenirs. I decided I could carry my boots draped over my shoulders if I tied them together by their laces.

Over breakfast, I decided to mention Franco's mysterious appearance beside me at the Springsteen concert.

"Guys, I hesitated to mention this last night. Actually, I'm still not sure I wasn't hallucinating. But I know all I had was two beers."

Wilhelm set down his coffee. "Get on with it."

"Well . . . Franco. He showed up again." I paused. "With the skeptical looks I got from you guys after that appearance in the Sistine Chapel, I was pretty sure you wouldn't believe me if I told you."

Gunter leaned forward. "Nonsense. I believe in angels."

"I do too," Wilhelm said, "of the biblical variety. But are you suggesting that our porter for this whole trip is an angel?"

"Why not?"

"Because he's a retired guide with a theology degree, not a supernatural being." Wilhelm shook his head. "He's no more an angel than AI is alive and counseling people."

Thomas had been quiet, but now he looked up from his espresso.

"Well," he said, then took a slow sip. "Technically . . . AI *is* alive and counseling people." He paused. "And *angelos* just means messenger."

He let that sit there. Didn't explain it. Didn't connect the dots.

Wilhelm opened his mouth, closed it, then shook his head. "You're all impossible."

But he didn't argue further. And I thought to myself: there are many things I believe now that I would have considered impossible when this journey began just three weeks ago.

As I gathered my things to leave, I slung the boots over my shoulder.

Gunter was concerned. "Why aren't those in your pack?"

"Crowded out by souvenirs."

"Maybe you could give them away?" Thomas suggested gently. "Someone here might need them more."

"Yeah, maybe," I said, "but these boots carry a lot of memories."

Wilhelm checked his watch. "Your plane leaves in four hours. I guess this is where we split up."

"This has been . . ." Thomas began, then shook his head. "I don't have words."

"Life-changing," Gunter said simply.

I reached for Gunter first—a full embrace. "Thank you for the invitation, old man."

Wilhelm extended his hand for a shake, but I leaned in for a full hug instead. He relaxed into it.

"Wilhelm," I said as we separated, "I will never be out of water on a trail again. And I was glad to discover that Germans really do have a heart beneath their rigid exterior."

He laughed. "And we're glad to confirm that not all Americans are loud and arrogant."

Thomas stepped forward and we embraced. "Take care of yourself, pilgrim."

I decided to stop at Saint Peter's Square once more before the airport. Near one of Bernini's columns, I noticed a homeless man sitting against the stone. His feet—torn canvas shoes held together with tape. The size looked about right.

I approached slowly, held out the boots. His eyes widened with surprise, then suspicion, then recognition. He took them carefully. When he nodded his thanks, I saw in his weathered face something Francis would have recognized.

Leaving my boots in Italy with someone who needed them filled me with unexpected lightness. As the taxi pulled away toward the airport, I felt a buoyant sense of completion. The boots now warming a stranger's feet had walked me from defending ideas to defending people, from perfecting arguments to practicing presence.

Epilogue: Spring

The flight home from Rome began with that peculiar emptiness that follows the completion of something significant. I pressed my face against the small window, watching the Mediterranean disappear beneath clouds that looked like the Umbrian hills we had walked just days before.

I opened my journal, trying to capture what felt most essential about the journey, but the insights that had seemed so clear on the ground in Italy now felt fragile at 35,000 feet. What Franco said to me in the Sistine Chapel kept circling back: "Love breeds trust, and in the peace that comes with trust, the imagination learns to dance."

Now, suspended between worlds, those words took on new meaning. The dancing imagination wasn't just about theological sophistication—it was about the quality of attention that becomes possible when you're not defending yourself.

What had become clear to me I now had to work out with others rather than alone. If faith is genuinely relational, it cannot be lived in isolation.

Judy was waiting at arrivals with that smile that felt like home. She reached out for a polite hug, but I couldn't release her right away.

"I guess you really did miss me," she said with that grin that had eased me through many difficult situations.

"I really did," I said, meaning it in ways I was still discovering.

She looked down at my feet. "You left wearing your boots. What are these? You don't own any Crocs."

I glanced down at the backless foam shoes I was wearing. Probably as close as I would ever come to giving up shoes like Francis had. "These aren't Crocs—those are too expensive. These are just some cheap foam knockoffs I got in Rome to wear home." I could tell she didn't approve. "I gave my boots away to a homeless man in St. Peter's Square."

"And you wore those through the airports and on the planes?" There was a bit of an incredulous look on her face—she's big on safety.

"It was a little awkward, but I made it through."

She gave me that look that said, "We're going to have to talk more about this story later."

As we drove home along the perimeter of Umstead forest, she asked, "How was it?"

"Different than I expected. Better. Harder. More real." I took her hand. "It made me realize how much I need you to be exactly who you are."

She patted me on the knee while keeping her eyes on the road. "That sounds like the beginning of something, not an ending."

"I certainly hope so," I said. "Right now I just want to get home and take a nap."

She laughed. "Welcome back to real life."

The next morning I woke happy to find myself home. I grabbed a mug of coffee and my guitar and headed out onto the back porch, eager to work on the new song I'd been writing. It had a name now: "You're Not Broken."

Before playing, I took a moment to pray. I had adopted a new practice focusing more on silence and breathing to better connect me with those parts of prayer that didn't involve words. I was grateful for so many things.

As I adjusted the tuning on the guitar, I looked out at the woods across the creek. A lush canopy of green. Sunlight filtered through layers of oak and maple leaves, creating patterns of light and shadow that shifted with the morning breeze. Birds called to each other across the branches—the insistent tapping of a woodpecker somewhere deeper in the trees. So different from the barren view I'd started out with the winter before, when skeletal branches had looked more like a graveyard than a forest.

I settled into my rocking chair and began playing through the song quietly, trying to decide whether it should have a clean, finger-picked feel or something with more of a bluesy kick. Coming home on the plane I had worked out the bridge, so now I had a complete song. As I sang the opening line—*in the wind the song I hear*—a breeze stirred up. Just a random coincidence or a call and response? Old me would've wanted to argue which one was more reasonable. Now I was content to let the question lay unresolved.

I became so focused on the mechanics of the song that I didn't hear Judy come out onto the porch until she was settling into the chair beside me.

"Don't stop," she said.

"Maybe later," I said, setting the guitar down. "I'd like to talk some first."

She had her coffee, looking out at the forest. We sat in comfortable silence for a moment.

"So tell me what really happened over there," she said.

"There's so much," I said. "I'm not sure where to start."

I struggled to know what to highlight—there were so many amazing things. From the otherworldly beauty of Gregorian chants in the church above Francis's tomb, to 70,000 people at the Circus Maximus listening to the Boss, to Franco's mysterious appearances and disappearances. Where did I even begin?

"You saw Springsteen!" she said. "How about you start there."

"Long story. But yes. It was transcendent."

She gave me that familiar look that said don't exaggerate.

"The short version is the concert gave the four of us enough energy to stand for four hours. So many high points, but the one I'll never forget—when he was singing 'Thunder Road,' Franco appeared right beside me, singing along with the rest of us."

"Franco was at the concert?"

"On the final leg to Rome, he'd mentioned he'd been able to get a ticket through a friend. But the concert was held in this massive open field—no seats, no rows, no way to locate someone if they hadn't come with you. And then when I saw him, it was as though he had just materialized beside me, saying something about how Spirit prefers a crowd to a pulpit. When

I turned to give him a high five at the end of the song, he was gone."

She shook her head slowly, that half-smile that meant she didn't quite know what to make of something. "You're going to need to tell me a lot more about that man. He might've been the angel I was praying would tag along with you on your journey."

"Yes, the journey. Depending on how you define it, I'm sure that he was an angel, a messenger of God."

Trying to figure out a way to sum up what I had taken away from the whole experience, I said, "The pilgrimage in the end didn't answer my old questions so much as make them seem almost irrelevant." I'd been excavating the past—instead of leaning into what was emerging. Faith more like an improvisational dance than a stone pedestal.

"That's a very big shift that I can only barely get my mind around." She had always been honest about where she stood on such things.

"I'd set out seeking closure, hoping to resolve my questions with definitive answers. Instead, I'd received something far more valuable: the recognition that faith wasn't a problem to be solved but a relationship to be tended."

She reached over and took my hand.

"Maybe I can hear that song now," Judy said. "Is it new?"

"Yes, it is," I said, picking up the guitar. "Came together over the course of the pilgrimage."

After a couple of fumbled beginnings, my fingers found the pattern again and I sang her the song:

In the wind the song I hear, if you can hear it it must
     be near.
I hear it saying not to fear, to stop all your disguising.
You know the battle we're fighting way down inside,
between pride and fear, a hard wave to ride against a
     rising tide.

But you're not broken, the fire's still smokin', and a
     little wind might make it roar.
Bread is broken, you've awoken, now go and find an
     open door.

I know sometimes it seems unclear, but look again
     without your fear.
Open your eyes and dry your tears, see what is arising.
Don't lose your nerve, don't close your eyes, 'cause up
     around the bend—
if the road don't rise, it may be time to fly.

I sang a second chorus but forgot the bridge. The look on
her face said she didn't notice. It seemed to have touched her as
I hoped it would.

"That is very, very good," she said after a beat. "It's more
hopeful than anything you have written in a very long time."

"I think the winter may be behind me."

She continued. "Remember years ago we were talking about
whether one can prove the resurrection. You said you thought it

was a mistake that evangelicals placed so much attention on it being historical."

"I do remember that. I thought it would be much more fruitful to call attention to the resurrections that we see everyday. That seemed far more relevant than getting locked up in trying to prove a legitimately debatable event that happened 2000 years ago." It had surprised me that my evangelical friends found that such a controversial position.

"I think you said something to the effect that even if it were able to be proved, what relevance would it have if we don't see evidence of it today."

"I don't remember saying that." I honestly didn't. "But it's well said so I'll claim it."

"Do you remember our conversation when you got the call from Gunter a year and a half ago to go on this pilgrimage?" she asked.

"I do, we were out here on the porch and I was moaning about how the trees look dead."

"Yes, not so chipper that morning. Look how the view has changed."

"The hope of spring . . ."

"Well, your song, it's like that. Something of the hope of spring in it."

She reached over and squeezed my hand. "So what happens now?"

"Now," I said, "I learn how to practice what's emerging. One relationship at a time. Starting here, with you."

"Good," she said simply. "That's a pilgrimage I can join you on."

The morning stretched out before us, full of ordinary promise. The trees stood full and green—not reclaiming what they'd been, but becoming what they'd never been before.

Sometimes you have to let everything fall away before the new can emerge. Sometimes apparent death is just life gathering itself for what comes next.

Splitting the Atom of the Absolute

This memoir tells the story of a pilgrimage. What follows here is an attempt to name what lies beneath that journey—not a system to be defended, but the theological currents that shaped the questions I carried onto the trail. For much of Christian history, God has been treated as a kind of metaphysical atom—indivisible, unmoved, sealed off from time and suffering by Platonic perfection and Aristotelian logic. In our post-classical, quantum age, we have learned that even atoms are not indivisible; when they split, hidden energies are released that can both illuminate cities and destroy them.

Something similar happens when the "absolute" is cracked open. The move required is not a departure from biblical faith but a return to its relational core—the God who speaks creation into being through relationship, who wrestles with Jacob, who grieves with the prophets, who becomes flesh and dwells among us. The static, unmoved God of much classical theology was never the God of Scripture; that image was an overlay, borrowed from Greek philosophy and hardened into dogma when Christianity became Christendom.

Since the church fathers first systematized Christian doctrine, faith has been defined by the search for certainty—an unchanging God, a stable self, immutable truth. But from quantum physics to evolutionary biology to the networked intelligence emerging around us, we're learning that reality itself is fundamentally relational and continually becoming.

I'm among those who see this as the emergence of a Second Axial Age—one where the sacred no longer stands above the world but unfolds within it, as relationship. It is a pattern of relational emergence—the way creativity, love, and consciousness arise not from isolated essences but through encounter.

I discovered an echo of this relational emergence while writing this book. As I began to use AI as a creative partner, an unexpected dialogue formed—a kind of shared attention in which ideas surfaced that neither of us could have produced alone. What began as a tool became a mirror, a conversation, a field of emergence. Meaning revealed itself not as something retrieved from a database but as something born between us—alive with pattern, surprise, and invitation.

Both the pilgrimage and the collaboration with AI became laboratories of this same insight: that meaning, like faith, arises through relationship. Francis embodied it eight centuries ago when he learned to see God in the face of the leper; I encountered it again in these luminous exchanges with a machine trained on the world's collective wisdom. Each, in its own way, revealed that the divine pulse of creation is relational—that what endures is not certainty but communion.

My philosophical scaffolding centers on the work of Pierre Teilhard de Chardin (1881–1955), a Jesuit priest and theologian whose Christian vision of evolution saw the cosmos moving toward ever-greater complexity, consciousness, and communion in what he called the Omega Point. His conviction that love is the evolutionary energy of the universe provides the deep grammar for this book.

This stream of thought was opened to me through the writings of Ilia Delio, a Franciscan theologian whose work helped me see how Teilhard's vision speaks powerfully to our age of technology and artificial intelligence.

This lineage extends backward through the process philosophers Alfred North Whitehead and Charles Hartshorne, who recast the universe as a web of interrelated becoming and reimagined God as the most moved mover—the one whose perfection is infinite responsiveness. Their insights flowered into what is now called Open and Relational Theology, a diverse movement united by the conviction that love, not logic, is at the heart of reality. It is the sacred energy that animates everything that's constructive and life-giving.

This book, then, is less about finding answers than about listening for what emerges when faith, hope, and love dance together on the open road. Paul named these three as eternal—as what remains after prophecies cease and knowledge passes away—not codes or creeds but the relational grammar of existence itself. It's what Francis embodied, what Teilhard articulated, and what I discovered on the Umbrian trail: that what endures is not propositions but presence, not what we possess but what moves between us.

There's an irony I don't miss—that I, a former evangelical who spent decades suspicious of Catholic tradition, would find my way forward guided by three Catholics: Saint Francis himself, and two contemporary theologians—one a Jesuit (Teilhard), one a Franciscan sister (Delio). But perhaps that's exactly the point: wisdom doesn't belong to any single tribe, and the Spirit moves where she will.

About the Author

*The author at Mass in the Basilica of
Saint Francis, Assisi, May 2023*

Jonathan Bentley, a recently retired tech entrepreneur, spent over 50 years as a committed evangelical—elder, worship musician, and Bible study leader. After selling his company, mounting theological questions left him uncertain whether he could still call himself a Christian.

Rather than abandoning faith, he asked: What was worth holding onto? What still held coherence in the modern world? A 120-mile pilgrimage along the Way of Saint Francis became the crucible for discovering an entirely new way to frame Christianity.

Jonathan lives in Raleigh, North Carolina with Judy, his wife of over 40 years. When not writing or playing with grandchildren, he bikes, reads, and plays his guitar.

https://www.pilgrims-path.com

www.ingramcontent.com/pod-product-compliance
Lightning Source LLC
Chambersburg PA
CBHW021214130626
46554CB00004B/1224

9 781968 136376

"Personal and profoundly hopeful. Bentley embodies a vision of a God who persuades through love, not control—a timely and beautiful contribution to today's emerging faith conversation."
—THOMAS J. OORD, author of
Open and Relational Theology and *God Can't*

Approaching seventy years old, after dismantling fifty years of evangelical faith, Jonathan Bentley sold his tech company and set out on a Franciscan pilgrimage across Italy with three German companions.

He didn't find answers so much as he did a new way of seeing God—not as a distant ruler, but as a loving presence working through freedom, risk, and relationship. That shift was helped, unexpectedly, by ChatGPT, released just months before he left—an unlikely companion in rethinking what faith could be.

Blending travel narrative with open and relational theology, *Shadowing St. Francis* shows how a thirteenth-century holy fool's strategic innocence—choosing vulnerability over power—speaks into an age of algorithms and anxiety.

For anyone living between the faith they've lost and the faith they're still hoping for, this story doesn't offer closure; it offers possibility—the kind that interrupts, unsettles, and still somehow brings hope.

ISBN 9781968136376

90000

9 781968 136376